SIGRID SANGL

BIEDERMEIER
TO BAUHAUS

Photographs by
**Barbara and
René Stoeltie**

HARRY N. ABRAMS, INC., PUBLISHERS

Original German manuscript translated by Niccola Sherman

Library of Congress Catalog Card Number: 00–104856
ISBN 0-8109-5708-6

BIEDERMEIER TO BAUHAUS was edited, designed, and produced
by Frances Lincoln Limited, London

Published in 2001 by Harry N. Abrams, Incorporated, New York

Printed and bound in Singapore

Harry N. Abrams, Inc.
100 Fifth Avenue
New York, N.Y. 10011
www.abramsbooks.com

Page 1 The restrained geometry of late
Jugendstil, which has moved away from its
early sinuous curves, is evident in the detailing
of the President's Reception Room in the
government buildings in Bayreuth, which
were designed by the Rank brothers in 1904.

Previous pages Ebonized Biedermeier furniture
from Vienna, Gothic-style wall decorations,
and softly draped muslin window dressing are
characteristic features of Schloss Rosenau, the
summer palace of the Dukes of Coburg, which
was built and decorated in 1814–19.

These pages Decorated in 1826–9, the central
dining room at the Charlottenhof, the summer
palace of the Crown Prince of Prussia, is a
prime example of the Classical style of the
architect Schinkel.

INTRODUCTION

Given the surfeit of publications on the historical interiors of France and England, it might seem astonishing that there has so far been no equivalent on Germany. But it becomes less surprising when one considers Germany's complicated history: for centuries the name of the country did not signify an area within recognizable borders, let alone a nation state with a distinctive cultural identity.

In this book Germany refers loosely to the area that is now the political entity, but includes the northernmost reaches of Austria. In the sixteenth century the German Nation was made up of a hundred or so individual duchies and principalities with varying degrees of autonomy. By the eighteenth century there were over three hundred such states. All the rulers were vassals of the Habsburg emperors who presided over the mighty Holy Roman Empire (its full title was 'The Holy Roman Empire of the German Nation') that embraced not just its ancestral territories of Austria and Germany, but also Burgundy, the Netherlands, Spain and its colonies and large parts of Italy. The area that spoke German included more land that is in present-day Austria, Italy, France and Switzerland. This explains why we can speak of a German language area but not of a politically or stylistically unified nation state. The latter only came about in the twentieth century, following political unification in 1870.

Unlike its centralized European neighbours, Germany lacked a common capital city to look to for leadership in matters of style. There were of course places where influential patrons and craftsmen lived, but the importance of these ebbed and flowed throughout the centuries according to changing economic conditions. Nevertheless, entirely original – and in some cases even bizarre – ways of decorating and furnishing a room emerged in various regions. Many of these developments not only contributed to the shaping of a German decorative tradition but were also in time adopted into the design vocabulary of other countries. It is these innovative trends that are the chief focus of this book.

German decorative style first blossomed early in the sixteenth century. For the next hundred years the wealthy trading centres of southern Germany, especially Augsburg and Nuremberg, were famous throughout Europe for their fine handcrafted goods – exquisite collector's cabinets, ornate wall panelling and wood-inlay designs, luxurious silverware and intricate clocks and automata. Under the patronage of the Habsburgs these *objets* were exported far and wide, together with accompanying pattern books which, reproduced as volumes of engravings, served as models for other makers. Then, in 1618, the Thirty Years' War broke out. With its almost total devastation of the German lands, it brought not just these trades, but all means of creativity, to a halt for half a century.

The so-called Fugger room at Schloss Tratzberg (**left**) reveals the prevalence of simple wooden panelling in the homes of the Renaissance period, while painted and silver-gilt floral carvings such as these at the Amalienburg in Munich (**centre**) indicate the prominent role of nature in eighteenth-century Rococo interiors. The ancient world in all its incarnations was the chief inspiration for the Neo-Classical period, as illustrated in the Etruscan Cabinet of Schloss Ehrenburg in Coburg (**right**).

The second half of the seventeenth century was a period of post-war regeneration, and decorative style embraced European influences, first from Italy and later from France, which was then the undisputed arbiter of taste, with its magnificent court at Versailles which many a German prince strove to imitate. The Rococo of southern Germany and of Potsdam, however, with its fantastical imitations of nature, was a unique departure in the history of interior design; it had no counterpart in the rest of Europe. And while Neo-Classicism was a pan-European movement, its German form was unhampered by the heavy, imitative French styles of Empire and Restoration; instead, it was associated with the theories of the country's great minds and literary giants, and is regarded as the embodiment of the intellectual and philosophical history of Germany. The perceived simplicity of its 'Biedermeier' phase has had a deep and lasting influence throughout the western world.

The interiors of nineteenth-century Germany were inspired both by Romanticism and its rejection of worldly concerns, and, more critically, by struggles for political unification. Contemporary decor was characterized by a search for the 'true' German style that was thought to exist in idealized memories of Gothic cathedrals and the aristocratic ways of the Renaissance. Jugendstil, which followed towards the end of the century, and which began as a conscious rejection of the historical styles of the nineteenth century, developed into one of the three most significant advances in applied arts on the path towards modern living. The other two were the English Aesthetic Movement and French Art Nouveau, which blossomed at the same time and along similar lines. The Werkstätten movement, an experiment with mass production unique to Germany, and the approach to modern design implicit in the foundation of the Bauhaus school, belong to the international history of twentieth-century design.

This book is not a history of interior style in Germany. Instead, touching only briefly on the familiar, Europe-wide trends, each chapter concentrates on developments that were specific to Germany, and shows interiors that demonstrate the variety and originality of German decor throughout the centuries. Since the overriding concern of the book has been for authenticity, all the rooms selected for inclusion are as true to their period as possible. None are museum reconstructions or installations 'in the style of ...'.

Just as a room acquires meaning only through an account of the desires and intentions of its occupants and creators, so too an impression of an interior's mood is essential to understanding it as a whole. By succeeding in capturing the essence of each room at the same time as they present its physical featuers, the book's photographers have made a magnificent contribution to a broadly unknown and revealing chapter in the history of European interior style.

Nostalgia for the great moments of German history played a central role in the historicist period of the nineteenth century, as illustrated in the castle of Marienburg (**left**). The elaborate fireguard designed by van de Velde in the Nietzsche Archive is characteristic of the *fin-de-siècle* Jugendstil artists' insistence on attention to the smallest detail (**centre**). The naïve piety and delight in bright colours evident in the decoration of this dowry cupboard were two of the features of nineteenth-century rural tradition (**right**).

THE
ℑnfluence of the
ℜenaissance

*The roots of German style
in the sixteenth century*

The fully panelled private rooms
in the fortress of Hohensalzburg
were extravagantly decorated in
the early years of the sixteenth
century (see pages 20–3).

Left An example of the highly naturalistic carvings on the painted and gilded built-in wall seats at Hohensalzburg. Hunting was one of the favourite occupations of the Prince-Bishop of Salzburg, who commissioned the lavish decoration of the living quarters in his fortress at the beginning of the sixteenth century.

Right The two circular alabaster reliefs portraying the Habsburg Emperor Maximilian II (d. 1576) and his wife were hung on the panelled walls of Schloss Tratzberg as a visible symbol of the allegiance owed to them by the inhabitants of the Schloss. The realism of the portraits was new at the time; it came with ideas about art and architecture that spread across the Alps from Italy.

Although there are very few surviving late medieval and Renaissance interiors in Germany – the examples in museums are mostly nineteenth-century reconstructions – there is enough evidence to show that a style of decor that we now recognize as discernibly German emerged during the fifteenth and sixteenth centuries. It was a time of relative prosperity and therefore of new buildings, especially in the south, and stylistic influences from Europe were absorbed and fashioned by the availability of local building materials – wood and iron – and by prevailing climatic conditions into interiors with a distinctively German flavour. Although rooms were not considered worth recording for their own sake, and genre painting was not yet invented, contemporary surroundings were often used as the background in religious pictures, particularly in panel paintings after 1520. Surviving documents, including inventories, also reveal a great deal about the contents of houses; and while there are few written accounts of domestic life of the period, the *Diary of a Journey through Italy, Switzerland and Germany in the Years 1580 and 1581* by the French philosopher and traveller Michel de Montaigne is crammed with enthralling details and meticulous observations – down to particulars of bed hangings and varieties of bread – of everyday life. It presents a picture of a country and a population that were thriving.

In the sixteenth century, of the hundred or so small states that made up the area that is now Germany, broadly those in the north-west were ruled by the princes of the Church, the bishops and abbots, while those in southern Germany were divided between the Wittelsbach and Habsburg families,

and those in the middle between the Wettins and the Hohenzollerns of Brandenburg. The wealth of the prince-rulers and the nobility varied enormously, as did their levels of education and standards of living, and the size of their states. The Elector of Saxony was the wealthiest; his lands were rich in minerals that fuelled the economy, the blossoming of which culminated in the splendour of his Dresden Residenz. Other rulers whose estates were not blessed with such natural resources, among them the dukes of Bavaria, raised incomes by levying taxes on consumer goods and luxuries that ranged from brandy, clothing and beer to salt and playing cards. In general the south, especially the Tyrol and what is now German-speaking Switzerland, was more prosperous than the north where the aristocracy tended their feudal estates with serf labour in distinctly unluxurious surroundings. Many still lived like the robber barons of an earlier age, in draughty castles among a rabble of battle-hungry companions who were not above ambushing passing merchant trains. However, inside the northern towns of the Hanseatic League (an association between trading centres formed in the thirteenth century, first by Hamburg and Lübeck, as a means of self-protection), the burghers had grown wealthier, more independent and more powerful than their contemporaries elsewhere.

In general there were no great differences between the ways of life in bourgeois homes and at court. Family and servants lived and slept together in the few heated rooms of the house or castle in fairly basic conditions. Real social differences only began to appear with the growth of ceremonial court tradition during the sixteenth century,

Left The realism of the sculptural decoration of these wooden portals, dating from after 1564, in the Lüneburg Rathaus betrays the pervasive influence of the Renaissance in Germany.

Right New ideas on depicting perspective, which had been developed by artists in Italy, filtered their way north across the Alps during the sixteenth century thanks to the proliferation of engravings of their work. These ideas were soon absorbed by south German craftsmen, and cabinet-makers began to decorate chests and coffers with fantastic inlay designs in intricate architectural motifs. Augsburg was the principal centre of this technique, for which the city became famous throughout Europe.

and even then clothing remained a better indication of social standing than the furnishings of a house until the eighteenth century. The first female couturiers were in business in Leipzig in 1640, whereas professional interior designers did not appear until the beginning of the twentieth century.

Considering how arduous travel was at that time, the influences from France, Spain, Italy and the Netherlands that touched on the everyday lives of German people were far more significant than we might imagine. Merchants from Augsburg and Nuremberg maintained trading links with the Middle East and the Ottoman Empire through an agency in Venice, and established their own bases as far afield as Goa on the west coast of India. They functioned as pearl traders in Seville and as creditors to the King of Portugal; they operated out of Antwerp and Amsterdam; and from the towns of the Hanseatic League on the Baltic coast they traded with Scandinavia and Russia. All these lines of communication brought the finest works of art and craft into Germany. Majolica came from Urbino, faïence from Delft, embossed leather wallcoverings from Venice, silks from Lucca and classical sculpture from Rome. Designs for ornament and furniture also arrived which, through reproduction by German engravers, formed the basis for an indigenous and highly refined style of decoration and craftsmanship. Nor was the cultural traffic all one-way. Because of the dynastic ties of their rulers and the far-reaching tentacles of the House of Habsburg, carpenters from Augsburg and Nuremberg travelled to Madrid, Florence and even London. By the end of the sixteenth century a flourishing, cosmopolitan class of craftsmen had established itself, most notably in Augsburg

and Nuremberg, which provided designs and furnishings for the most beautiful rooms in Bavaria – and far beyond – well into the seventeenth century. The most important exports were the Augsburg collector's cabinets, famed for their finely decorated fronts and numerous internal drawers. Chiefly through the marketing efforts of the art dealer Philipp Hainhofer these became some of the most prized pieces of furniture in the courts of Europe.

With the artefacts that came into Germany from across the Alps towards the beginning of the sixteenth century arrived a new approach to living space. Wandering scholars and collectors educated in the humanities brought with them the ideas of the Italian Renaissance. In the more prosperous south, wealthy nobles began to abandon their fortresses in the countryside and build themselves town palaces. And in the towns, cramped conditions, narrow winding staircases and dark rooms gave way to spacious arcades and lighter, airier dwellings. In the second half of the century these ideas were taken up with great enthusiasm by the bourgeois families who had amassed fortunes as financiers to the nobility. Upwardly mobile and newly ennobled, they used their wealth to build houses in the latest fashions, seeking to emulate the culture and lifestyle of their patron-princes. The grand rooms of the Fuggers' Augsburg residence, which was decorated by the Italian-influenced Friedrich Sustris between 1569 and 1573, were fitted with marble, for example, and were 'the most elaborate rooms I have ever seen', according to Montaigne. Favourite features in other houses of theirs included decorative floral wall paintings with allegorical motifs and complicated fountains.

These wealthy families also played a crucial role in the financial prosperity of Germany during this period. Through the dealings of the Fugger family, for example, Augsburg grew into the undisputed financial capital of Christendom. Formerly cloth merchants, they financed the Habsburg Emperor Maximilian's war in Italy, took part in the trade in Catholic indulgences and were instrumental – by the size of their bribes – in electing Charles V as Emperor. They controlled the enormously profitable silver mining enterprises of the Tyrol, and they also owned silver, copper and lead mines, and held a worldwide monopoly in copper.

The bankruptcy of the Habsburg creditors at the end of the sixteenth century led to a decline in the fortunes of merchants like the Fuggers. But by then the ideas of the Italian Renaissance had spread throughout Germany and had had an impact on the interiors of both bourgeoisie and nobility in both country and towns. And then in 1618 came the Thirty Years' War. It was to prove catastrophic for Germany, setting its cultural clock back by several decades.

Among the finest surviving houses of the sixteenth century in southern Germany are Schloss Tratzberg, which contains many of the elements that would have been typical of a wealthy bourgeois home, and has an especially notable collection of late-Gothic and early Renaissance furniture, and Hohensalzburg, the sumptuous living quarters of the Prince-Bishop of Salzburg (see page 21).

Schloss Tratzberg, which lies to the north of Innsbruck in the middle of the lush corridor of the Tyrol, was built in 1500 by the Tänzl family (it passed into the ownership of the Fuggers in 1589) who had made a large fortune through

mining and used the house as a showcase of their wealth and status. Its many generously proportioned rooms were lined with skilfully worked panelling, lit by large windows, and featured fine, marble doorways, magnificent ironwork, beautifully grained burr-wood and ornate low-relief carving. The intricately interlaced iron doormounts and the finely carved crests above each door reveal an unprecedented approach to the design of a building: every aspect, from the architectural shell to the decorative details of the interior, was conceived as part of an integral whole.

The rooms were unusually large for a private residence of the time. The sheer size of a room had long been a clue to the wealth of its owner: the larger the span of a floor, the longer the supporting beams had to be, requiring expensive wood from rare, tall, mature trees. The largest beams were frequently decorated in fine detail, as they are in Schloss Tratzberg where they are supported by delicately carved marble columns. The recent invention of Butzenscheiben, or bulls-eye panes – thick discs of glass which were fitted together with lead to form larger areas – was another reason for the large size of the rooms, as the bigger windows made possible by this technique let considerably more light into a room.

Opposite An opening above one of the splendid marble doorways at Schloss Tratzberg allows heated air to pass from one room to the next. The large expanse of glass in the windows, which let in an unusual amount of light for a domestic interior, is an indication of the wealth of the residents.
Above Schloss Tratzberg looks out over the valley of the Inn river. A fourth wing was added after 1560 to form a vast quadrant and the arcaded façades of the inner courtyard were painted in *c.* 1570 in new Italian Renaissance style, with garlands of fruit, marbled pinnacles and Latin *bons mots*.

Many of the unpanelled ceilings and walls of Schloss Tratzberg are painted. The ceiling of the oriel off the so-called Fugger room is adorned with gold stars against a blue background. This was a favourite theme of the time, not least because it was a means of showing off wealth: the gold and the ultramarine pigment used for the sky were both vastly expensive. It is reported of the cost-conscious Nuremberg burgher Tucher that in 1511 he painstakingly counted the stars on the hall ceiling of his town house to check that the full four hundred had indeed been applied as instructed. Another popular motif, for walls, was patterns of roses and creeping vines and tendrils, such as the ones that Paul Behaim requested for his parlour in Nuremberg. Other especially fine examples can be seen today in the so-called 'green rooms' at the castles of Churburg, in the Tyrol, and of Reifenstein, in that part of the Tyrol that is now in Italy.

While rooms for everyday use would be plain, white-washed by simple labourers every two years or so, the decor- ation of the grander rooms called for skilled craftsmen. Some of the most beautiful late fifteenth- and early sixteenth-century murals, such as those in the castles of Freundsberg or Friedberg, in the Tyrol, showing events from classical antiquity and illustrations of complete literary works, were the outcome of a highly successful marriage between German creative instinct and the humanist ideals adopted from Italy.

In the main hall of Schloss Tratzberg is a tempera mural of the family tree of the House of Habsburg that dates from the beginning of the sixteenth century. Its significance is far more than purely decorative. In the rich tradition of emperor worship, its scenes refer directly to the family's ties with their Habsburg rulers. It also makes the hall a precursor of the Kaisersaal of the Baroque age – a ceremonial banqueting hall in grand Catholic German houses which was furnished for a possible visit from the emperor. There are 148 almost life-sized half-figures painted in eye-catching detail – which are of great interest for their place in the history of costume – and the direct line from Rudolf I, the first Habsburg king, to Philip I, who became King of Spain in 1504, is decorated with a background of blue clouds. The way in which the genealogical lines are represented is also highly revealing of the patriarchal system: the female lines are shown as dry twigs and the male ones as lush green shoots.

Family trees and, even more so, coats of arms are some of the era's favourite decorative themes. There are famous examples in the castle of Churburg and in the fortress of Hohensalzburg. Montaigne describes how it was considered good form for travellers staying in German inns to leave behind a painting of their coat of arms, and reports with wry amusement: 'The Germans are in love with their coats of arms; for in every inn one finds scores of them left behind on the walls by passing noblemen, even every pane of glass is covered with them.'

The larger rooms at Schloss Tratzberg were warmed by ornate tiled stoves which tower in the corners; the smaller chambers next to them were warmed by air passing through little windows above the doors between the rooms. Generally stoves were the focal point of the main living room and, luckily for the inhabitants, the wash stand was customarily placed in the parlour, next to the stove. Stoves were typically made of iron in the north and tiled in the south, where the elaboration and the subject matter of the tiles were clues to the wealth and level of education of their owners. Sometimes these ceiling-high ovens would be inset with steps and

Above and right The main hall at Schloss Tratzberg, used only for ceremonial occasions, is decorated on all four walls with the family tree of the Habsburgs, to whom the Tänzl family owed their wealth and position. The scrolls beneath the figures give their names and their genealogical details. The slender marble column that supports the massive beam is carved to look like interwoven branches – an example of the naturalism of the late Gothic period.

Pairs of huge stags' antlers were embedded in the walls beneath the family tree and now serve as candelabra. When the painted beasts were added in the nineteenth century they must have had an extraordinarily naturalistic effect, especially in the evening when, in the flickering light, the stags looked as though they were about to step out of the walls.

niches, and became known as 'sofa' ovens because the warm tiles made a cosy seat.

The collection of original furniture at Tratzberg numbers among the most important from the period immediately after 1500. The living-room walls, panelled with Swiss pine, are lined with benches and, where these meet the doorways, each ends in a high armrest edged with a border of carved branches. Several of the benches take the form of chests, with the seats doubling as lids. The free-standing pieces of furniture – seats, chests, tables, grand two-tiered cupboards and four-poster beds – were decorated with carved tracery and branch and twig motifs, as well as with delicate pale maple veneers. Montaigne was continually struck by the abundant use of wood in Germany and claimed that in his entire journey he had not seen a single bedroom or dining room which was not panelled. He remarked upon the special finishes that the south German cabinet-makers had developed in the creation of furniture. 'Only pine is used for furniture and panelling, the most common type of wood in their forests; however it is carefully coloured, stained and cleaned, and they even use a special kind of hair brush to dust their benches and tables.' It was in fact the Augsburg cabinet-makers who in the second half of the sixteenth century perfected the technique of *intarsia*, whereby wall panels, and especially the fronts of chests and coffers, are inlaid with wood veneers stained in a variety of colours. At the time there was a vogue – again, in response to Italian ideas – for highly complex *trompe l'oeil* drawings of architectural ruins or multi-dimensional objects, and cabinet-makers showed off their expertise by reproducing these as designs on flat

furniture panels, chiefly on the fall-front writing surfaces of chest-like secretaires that were based on the Spanish *vargueños*. Augsburg chests with exquisite *intarsia* increasingly became collectors' items, and not only did they find their way along the trade routes over the Alps to Florence and Naples, but the cabinet-makers themselves also migrated there, making it difficult today to determine the exact provenance of one of these chests.

In the 1580s there came a new fashion for furniture with architectural and sculptural features in the form of columns, pilasters and cornices, and the study of the Classical Orders became an obligatory part of a cabinet-maker's training. Larger cupboards began to look increasingly like the façades of Classical buildings; these were appropriately named Fassadenschränke. The guilds of the imperial cities of south Germany, such as Nuremberg, Ulm and Augsburg, each developed their own variation of Fassadenschränke, but all used indigenous woods. A particular favourite for the front panels was Hungarian ash, which had a wave-like grain that enlivened the flat surfaces.

The beds in Germany gave rise to an extensive commentary from Montaigne and he claimed to detect national differences in people's attitudes to their beds: 'The German becomes ill if he has to sleep on a mattress, the Italian on feathers, the Frenchman without bed curtains or a fire in the hearth.' He also described the bases in the vicinity of Constanz: 'pallets filled with the leaves of a certain tree, which are more comfortable and longer lasting than those filled with straw'. As he passed through each Bavarian village he noted with characteristic meticulousness how while some houses had curtains hanging in the windows, the canopies and

---

Above The art of making cabinets with exquisitely worked *intarsia* reached a peak in Augsburg in the years leading up to 1600.
Opposite The furnishings and decor of Schloss Tratzberg reveal a good deal about the way of life there in the late Gothic period, as well as about the taste of a wealthy merchant family.
Opposite top left The sparsity of the furnishings is characteristic. The walls, panelled in Swiss pine, are inset with cupboards and lined with

benches. Decorative elements are provided by the lush fronds of ironwork and the elaborately carved crests over the doors that display the Tänzl family's coat of arms.
Opposite top right Because of the raw mountain climate, the wash stand with its pewter basin and towels was placed next to the tiled stove, which also heated water.
Opposite bottom left Four-poster beds – such as this one from 1615 – would have been hung

with curtains to keep out the draughts.
Opposite bottom right In these guest apartments, nominally for the emperor, the wood has been worked with iron combs to create an interestingly textured surface. Hanging from the wood-panelled ceiling is an 'illustrious woman' chandelier made from a set of antlers in the form of a woman's body. Designs for such objects were produced by distinguished artists, including Albrecht Dürer.

drapery that were an essential part of most French beds were frequently missing. Of the beds in German inns he complained, 'the pillows, which are the fashion there, have no covers; the only bedclothes are feather quilts, and they are distinctly unsalubrious'. Conditions may well have been different in such a wealthy household as Schloss Tratzberg, but in fact there were fewer variations in the level of cleanliness according to social status than one might assume. The construction of the beds that Montaigne described was much the same everywhere: 'Their beds are so high, that one generally needs steps to climb into them and almost everywhere there are smaller beds tucked under the bigger ones.' The steps by which one reached the bed often took the form of coffers, in which precious items were stored as well

as clothes. The smaller beds which Montaigne mentioned were intended for children and also for guests. They were usually set on rollers and became known as Rollbetten.

Textiles were naturally also an integral part of the furnishing of a grand residence such as Schloss Tratzberg. Since so many of the textiles have disappeared, the impression of the rooms today is often deceptively stark. Wall hangings were popular among the nobility by virtue of their portability. Rolled up and packed away they could be produced on a journey, on visits to other houses, or even on the battlefield, to provide a fittingly luxurious environment in a matter of minutes. These wall hangings often took the form of embroidered linen panels or woollen tapestries, made by the housewives themselves or purchased from

Left This little oriel chamber leads off a room in Schloss Tratzberg that was named by the Fugger family after Queen Anna of Bohemia although she never actually stayed here. The table, on which stands a wrought-iron bird cage, and the chairs date from after 1560, and are typical of the furniture that was made in Germany in the Renaissance style. The *intarsia* panel on the wall is unusually large; its scroll-work is in the manner of Cornelis Floris (who came from Antwerp and became famous for his innovative designs which combined scroll-work with cartouches). The block-printed wall hangings beneath the burr-wood rail, which are original to the room, would have helped to keep it warm.

Right Gothic tracery dominated the appearance of furniture during the first half of the sixteenth century. It could serve a practical use, as in the perforated panels of this four-poster bed, which allowed air into the enclosed, curtained interior, or be used purely decoratively, as on the panels on the drawers and door-fronts of this magnificent two-tiered cupboard. This imposing piece of furniture, now at Schloss Tratzberg, once belonged to a Knight of the German Order – a high-ranking medieval military association – and would have been used to store liturgical vestments. The chairs, which date from later in the century, are covered with the original leather, painted with naturalistic Renaissance-style floral patterns. The opening high in the wall to the left of the bed allowed for the circulation of warm air.

nunneries. In the early fifteenth century they were decorated chiefly with stylized vine tendrils and images of animals; figures of saints became popular later; and by 1600 large wall hangings were being embroidered with whole narrative sequences. The most costly wall hangings were the tapestries that originated in Brussels; most of those in the Habsburgs' collections portray classical or biblical scenes; and, enhancing both their value and their glimmering effect, the most elaborate ones contain many pounds of gold thread.

Inventories of bourgeois town houses show how widespread was the use of household textiles. During the fourteenth century German textiles had been the most sought-after in Europe, but the industry's fortunes had then declined and by the beginning of the sixteenth century woollen fabrics from the Netherlands were the most popular. These were used as hangings over the backs of panelled settles, as covers for cushions on benches and over draughty doorways. In wealthier households fine silks imported from Venice were hung as draperies over paintings and mirrors. Typical of beds throughout Germany were the blue-and-white checked or striped quilt covers, made in Cologne from a linen and cotton mix known as fustian, and dyed with colourfast blue woad. A taste for more elaborately decorated bed hangings, trimmed with braid, lace and embroidery, grew up during the sixteenth century. But the greatest value was given to tasselled silk bed hangings. These fabrics, generally more expensive than the structure of the bed itself, were sometimes taken on journeys and frequently passed down as heirlooms.

Table cloths, door curtains and even napkins (whose frequent absence from German inns was bemoaned by Montaigne) were also treasured by young housewives. The demand for textiles increased to such an extent that it led to the revival of the German textile industry. Augsburg became the leading centre of manufacture – fabric was printed there for the first time in 1524 – and weavers there were soon copying Flemish woollens as well as producing a great deal of linen.

Not far away from Schloss Tratzberg as the crow flies, but in a quite different Alpine valley, lies the fortress of Hohensalzburg. Within the castle are probably the most important surviving princely interiors of the pre-Renaissance period in the entire German-speaking area: the living quarters of Salzburg's prince-bishop, Leonhard von Keutschach. Dating from around 1502, the rooms have a more backward-looking, Gothic character than those at Schloss Tratzberg, and indeed von Keutschach was one of the last provincial princes to rule in the manner of a feudal knight, installing himself in noble surroundings high above the town in a heavily fortified castle. He retreated here whenever the local peasants and the miners (who were in dispute among themselves) became a threat. He extended the castle, making it into a self-sufficient stronghold which, if necessary, could withstand attacks from his unruly subjects below. And in the process of building, he had his coat of arms, a white mangelwurzel, emblazoned in more than fifty places on the walls and ramparts of the fortress around him.

The main room of von Keutschach's living quarters, on the upper floor of the castle's central residence, is the Goldene Saal, or Golden Hall. Panelled throughout, this large, stately room has a massive ceiling beam 17 metres (56 feet)

Left Salzburg's status-conscious Prince-Bishop Leonhard von Keutschach had every possible surface of his royal residence – erected in 1501 in the fortress of Hohensalzburg – adorned with his coat of arms, the mangelwurzel. It appears above the marble doorways of the Goldene Saal. With its deeply ribbed ogee arches, polished wood panelling and gold-studded ceiling, this vast room was designed to impress.

Above A view up to the royal residence in the castle's inner courtyard shows the addition of oriels. A new feature of the age, these allowed more light into the internal rooms than had previously been possible.

long held up by spiral columns of distinctively grained red marble from nearby Adnet. The Prince-Bishop had his beloved coat of arms painted on this beam, this time as a provocative political statement, his own arms holding the dominant position between those of the German electors and regional rulers. The coffered wooden ceiling is particularly fine. Painted a rich, deep blue and decorated with golden studs, it is reminiscent of the star-patterned ceilings in other great houses.

A splendid door with ornamental iron mounts in stylized flower and stem patterns leads the way into the Goldene Stube, or Golden Parlour, one of the most stunning of all secular rooms in Europe. Like the Goldene Saal, it is panelled from floor to ceiling and painted a striking, intense blue with ornamental gilded studs on the walls and coffered ceiling. The huge, lavish stove of 1501 is a showpiece of Salzburg craftsmanship, its colourful tiles embellished with figure reliefs.

Hidden away in an oriel off the Goldene Stube is a little chamber that is representative of a particular type of room adopted from the palaces of Renaissance Italy: a *studiolo*. The function of such tiny rooms is unclear: akin to a study, a place for quiet contemplation and concentration such as that depicted by Albrecht Dürer in his *St Jerome in his Study*, it was also a place to store books, precious objects and other memorabilia, as described by the fifteenth-century architectural theorist Alberti. Very probably there was once a desk in the *studiolo* at Hohensalzburg, on which the Prince-Bishop would keep his books, as well as chests and boxes for his collection of treasures. Lined with wood, this cubbyhole, with windows in its two outer walls, has had its panelling painted to resemble tapestries. The Hohensalzburg *studiolo* is one of the very few to have existed north of the Alps. The only comparable example is the one which the Fugger family – who were familiar with Italian palaces – built in 1546 next to the main reception room in their schloss at Donauwörth.

Next to the Goldene Stube lies the Prince-Bishop's bedroom, which is only slightly less grand and colourful than the Stube itself. Among the lavish carving in this room are some particularly beautiful figure reliefs that depict in great detail scenes from everyday life, such as hunting.

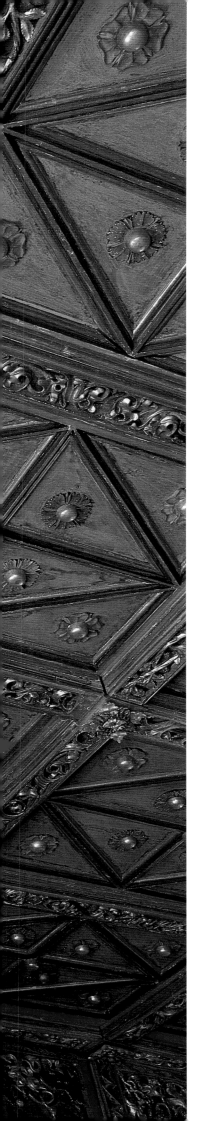

Left Despite a few nineteenth-century additions, the Goldene Stube at Hohensalzburg remains an exceptional example of late-Gothic domestic design. The lush tangles of gilded carving on the ceiling and wall panelling demonstrate German naturalistic ornament at its best.
Below left The built-in seating in a niche within the Goldene Stube would have been covered in sumptuous cushions. The *studiolo*, a small panelled chamber for the private use of the prince-bishop, is behind the internal window.
Below right The reliefs which decorate the vast, colourfully glazed stove in the Goldene Stube – which dates from *c.* 1501 – form an anthology of the Christian world view: around a central scene of the Coronation of the Virgin are gathered a collection of saints, prophets and apostles. Also represented are the most important German electors; the order in which they appear is indicative of the status and position which each was seen to hold. The wooden lions on which the stove appears to rest are purely ornamental: in fact the whole is built around an iron frame which is firmly set into the wall.

Little has remained of the furnishings of these rooms. None the less, from the surviving evidence it is not difficult to guess why they had such a fine reputation. Like all furnishings of the northern Alpine region, those at Hohensalzburg were made chiefly from the reddish-hued and densely knotted wood of the Swiss pine. The main ornamental feature is the densely interlaced tracery which evokes the stonework of a Gothic cathedral and breaks up the surfaces into a delightful play of finely woven shadows, with gilding providing the highlights. Many of the luxurious wall hangings have disappeared, but the Moorish tapestries that von Keutschach's successor brought from Spain – he had a dual role as bishop of Murcia as well as Salzburg – are still in place.

While the economic conditions in the south of Germany enabled building on as grand a scale as that of Schloss Tratzberg and Hohensalzburg to take place during the sixteenth century, those in the north were less favourable. The feudal lords rarely possessed the means to decorate their houses with any grandeur; and the burghers of the old towns of the Hanseatic League were increasingly losing their wealth as they lost their trading supremacy to English traders. Nevertheless some impressive examples of authentic urban German interiors have survived in this region.

The town hall in Lüneburg is a fine example of early bourgeois splendour. Lüneburg owed its wealth to the salt in its soil. Panned from the brackish waters, it was the only means of preserving food and so fetched high prices in the Hanseatic towns where it was traded as merchandise. This trade promised riches and gave confidence to the inhabitants of the town in the fourteenth century: they rid themselves of their ruling prince, storming his castle and tearing it down. Then they took the fortunes of the town into their own hands by founding a town council. Lüneburg grew into a prosperous and elegant city, as is still apparent in fifteenth- and sixteenth-century gabled brick houses. These houses survived because not only did the Guelph princes reconquer the town during the Thirty Years' War, but in addition competition from the foreign salt trade caused the town to loose its chief source of wealth and consequently all its significance in the eighteenth century. This loss of fortune and civic independence meant that there was little new building; thus the existing architecture was preserved, making Lüneburg one of the very few showcases of late-medieval and Renaissance secular interiors today.

Wood was the predominant building material as well as the defining feature of discriminating interiors in northern Germany just as it was in the south. The amount of skilled carpentry work was never as great in the north as it was further south, where built-in cupboards, coffers, benches and chests were an integral component of the wall cladding. Instead, the tradition of covering walls and ceilings with decorative painting was stronger and more widespread. Painted by itinerant artists, the themes were generally mythological or biblical; portraits of readily recognizable emperors, kings or philosophers were sometimes included, but family members were seldom portrayed as this was not part of the standard repertoires.

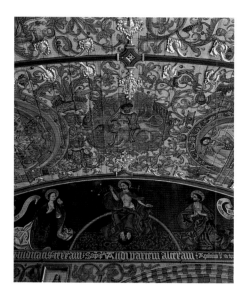

Left and above The great chamber of Lüneburg's Rathaus was used as the court room and also to receive guests and official visitors, for whom the precious collection of silver would be brought out. It was built in c. 1330; the barrel-vaulted wooden ceiling was installed in 1470, but the paintings of biblical scenes were not added until c. 1529.

Although many of the gabled houses of Lüneburg have parlours, hallways and even banqueting halls lined with wood and painted with decorative themes, the most beautiful rooms of the period belong to the town hall, the Lüneburg Rathaus. The Baroque façade belies the great age of the building – constructed of brick and half-timbering – behind it. The colourful floor tiles from 1330 in the main hall, the oldest surviving council chamber and court room in Germany, are a better clue. Broad and heavy in its proportions and sombre in mood, this imposing room is distinguished by its heraldic stained glass of 1478, its furnishings and its decorative painting. Although all the rooms of the Rathaus have painted wooden wall panelling and barrel-vaulted ceilings, the effect of these is particularly memorable in this public room. Allegorical scenes from Roman history, after woodcuts by Hans Burkmair and Hans Baldung Grien, make a fitting theme.

The principal pieces of furniture are the three so-called 'Schenkschieve', the north German version of the French buffet, used to display the town's collection of silver, chiefly ceremonial cups and platters. Schenkschieve were found not only in public rooms, but also in the private houses of any wealthy burgher of Lüneburg. They stood either in the entrance hall or in the main Stube, usually laden with pewter dishes, with silverware – which was enormously popular in the sixteenth and seventeenth centuries – and with drinking glasses – beer tankards and wine goblets – all set out for admiring visitors.

The rooms adjoining the great council chamber of the Lüneburg Rathaus – the Old Chancellery of 1433, the Electoral Chamber of 1457 and the Old Archive with its fittings of 1521 – can all be seen more or less in their original arrangement and colouring. The brass chandeliers, with a bowl at the centre, are typical of north Germany, and were also commonly found in the houses of the wealthier patricians. The benches running around the walls would have provided the principal seating at a time when freestanding chairs were still rare. They would have been spread with cushions for comfort and their backs lined with a type of patterned linen known as Rücklaken (or 'backsheets').

The surviving household inventories are the only means of forming a more complete picture of the interior of a bourgeois Lüneburg town house. From these we know that every room was panelled throughout. A tiled stove and a fireplace against the wall provided adequate heating for the family Stube (although the remains of a medieval underfloor heating system can be seen behind some cupboards in the Rathaus). One inventory of 1544 records suits of armour, shields and weapons hanging above the fireplace – a practice that could well have been the source of the nineteenth-century fashion for romanticized Gothic interiors with just such displays of armour.

The quantity of furniture in the houses of Lüneburg, as in the whole of northern Germany, was still relatively modest. Merchants would have had specific types of furniture designed to meet the requirements of business, such as special cupboards with small divisions for the innumerable different coinages that a trader was obliged to have in his house (until an imperial decree of 1559 limited the number of currencies within Germany to a total of thirty), and beneath the surface of a painted table might be a shelf for storing the account books. Family treasure was generally kept in the bedchamber, where everyone slept together. There would be a chest next to the bed filled with silver dishes and a box for the rings and jewels belonging to the lady of the house, as well as a cupboard for the household's supply of linen, costly fabrics and trimmings. Although there were few items of freestanding furniture, rooms were far more cluttered than we might conclude from surviving evidence. All the fabric items would also have given the room a lived-in feeling, and there would have been many smaller items of practical use, such as crockery and candlesticks, fire irons and so on, in the room, as well as dishes of brass and ceramic displayed on the mantelpiece.

Left top This room in the Lüneburg Rathaus, which was used for festivities, dates from the second half of the fifteenth century. Beneath the beamed ceiling, painted with a splendid array of portraits and coats of arms, are displayed several late-Gothic chandeliers, imaginatively constructed from antlers, wrought iron and figures of saints.
Left bottom The entrance to the Gewandhaus, or Garment House – used for the trading of cloth – at the Rathaus is guarded by a wrought-iron grille, in which its creator, Hans Ruge, proudly set his name in 1576. Such intricately cast iron-work is typical of the Renaissance art of Lower Saxony.
Right The merchants of Lüneburg stored their correspondence in the Old Archive. The structure of this room, completed in 1521, has survived virtually untouched. The cupboards, each marked with a capital letter, contain the scrolled documents, most complete with their original seals.

Baroque Grandeur and Rococo Fantasies

Nature as a model for interiors in the eighteenth century

The little pavilion of Amalienburg , which dates from 1734, is one of the most fanciful examples of German Rococo (see pages 34–7).

The depredations of the Thirty Years' War in the first half of the seventeenth century totally devastated Germany. The population was reduced by almost two-thirds. The economy was in ruins. No area of life was unaffected. Neither the aristocracy nor the middle classes could afford to commission furnishings, let alone fashionable or expensive ones, until the end of the century.

When the economy began to recover, money was spent firstly on churches – to re-establish the religious proclivities and alliances that had been the cause of the war in the first place. In Bavaria, where the electors held particularly strong links with the Pope and the Catholic Church, church and monastery building was influenced chiefly by the Baroque architecture of Rome, where the Baroque style had evolved at the end of the sixteenth century. As well as being seen in grand edifices such as the Theatiner Church in Munich, the style is most evident in many country pilgrim churches where heavy garlands of fruit, fantastically exaggerated scrolls, plump cherubs and fleshy swathes of acanthus leaves smother the walls. Originally the work of Italian craftsmen arriving from over the Alps or via Bohemia, the prime features of this German form of the Baroque were soon widely disseminated through the avidly received publication of highly detailed pattern books, printed in Augsburg or Nuremberg. The Italian influence on German Baroque is chiefly apparent in *trompe-l'oeil* ceiling paintings, which appear to give the viewer a glimpse into the heavens, and fabulously elaborate stucco decoration, heavy with acanthus leaf motifs. Some of the most opulent schemes can be seen at the old palace of Ehrenburg in

The interior design of grand German houses in the late seventeenth century was dominated by Baroque influences from Italy, seen particularly in the elaborate stucco work. Three rooms at Schloss Ehrenburg in Coburg dating from 1692 – the Giant Room (**left**), the Red Drawing Room (**centre**), and the Goblin Room (**right**) – have sumptuously decorated ceilings that include the typical acanthus leaf motifs, some of which were so heavy that they needed wood, wire and lead to support them. The Giant Room is named after the torch-bearing figures that visually support the ceiling.

Coburg. The style found little entry into bourgeois homes; the clergy remained its principal champions, in places of worship and, for those wealthy enough, in the field of palace architecture. Once the prince-bishops had the means to build new residences at the beginning of the eighteenth century, they looked to the art of the Viennese court, to which they were politically allied, for inspiration. Both Schloss Pommersfelden in Franconia and the palace of Würzburg include elements influenced by the great Belvedere Palace in Vienna. But at the same time specifically German decorative elements also began to emerge. These included the elaborate scrollwork that appeared as inlay adorning furniture as well as woven into tapestries and upholstery fabric. Some of the best examples can be seen at Schloss Pommersfelden, built between 1711 and 1718, the private residence of the prince-bishops of Schönborn, in Franconia, where the panelling of whole rooms is decorated with scrollwork marquetry. Pommersfelden also has one of the most beautiful 'cabinet of mirrors' in the whole of Germany and a grotto-like *sala terrena;* both illustrate the beginning of a new phase in interior decoration that led to the fantasies of German Rococo.

Throughout the eighteenth century the German states were politically torn between the two poles of Vienna and Paris; this had a ricochet effect on matters of taste and fashion. As late as the middle of the century the Empress of Austria is said to have forbidden the import of luxury French furniture to Vienna; and yet French style continued to reign supreme. Balthasar Neumann, the architect of the bishop's palace in Würzburg, travelled incognito to France in order to bring back examples of chairs which could then be copied by Franconian craftsmen. And the Bavarian elector Max Emanuel – who was forced to spend long years of exile in France because he had sided against Austria in the war – was so impressed by the splendour of the court of Versailles that he not only called Bavarian artists to Paris to be schooled in the French styles, but also on his return brought foreign artists home with him. Chief among these was François Cuvilliés the Elder. Cuvilliés trained as an architect in Paris although he had been born in the Walloon, where he had been court dwarf. He was to be chiefly responsible for the development of the uniquely German strand of Rococo which was distinguished from the more grandiose styles of Versailles by the fanciful use of natural forms. His designs, which were published by various engravers from 1738 and later by his son Cuvilliés the Younger, played a key role in the development of the style. Further north, in Berlin, its chief protagonists were the Hoppenhaupt brothers. Combined with a superabundant use of gilt and the newly fashionable mirrors, and often incorporating exotic elements, German Rococo dominated aristocratic interiors for most of the eighteenth century.

The craze for nature expressed in German Rococo knew no bounds: native and exotic natural forms – herons and reeds, palm fronds and gourds – were combined with cheerful abandon. Carved furniture was made to resemble tree trunks, fragile sofas seemed to consist entirely of twisted fronds of foliage, and chair backs were so covered with carved flower buds that the chairs were patently uncomfortable to sit on. Flat surfaces were embellished with marquetry designs in wood veneers of different grains reflecting the enthusiasm of cabinet-makers for the natural qualities of their materials. Elaborate stucco mouldings, often decorated with flower tendrils, were fixed to walls to make panels (sometimes these took the form of trellis populated by little papier-mâché birds), bringing the garden into the house. Grottoes were studded with semi-precious stones from the mountains and adorned with shells from German rivers. Looking glasses from the first German mirror factories were used to make the ultra-fashionable 'cabinets of mirrors'. These reflected garden views into inner rooms, so blurring the dividing line between indoors and outdoors. The sense of structure was further undermined by furniture forms that were so much part of the overall design that sometimes one could no longer see where a commode standing against the wall ended and the organic mouldings began.

Natural forms, epecially curving foliage, fragile stems and blooms and graceful shells, were the chief inspiration behind the German Rococo style. These were often placed against pale or delicately marbled backgrounds, as seen at the Altes Schloss outside Bayreuth (**left**) and at Schloss Mosigkau (**centre**). Blue and white contrasts and related chinoiserie designs also became fashionable, as seen at the Amalienburg palace (**right**).

A delight in changing levels of reality and an almost naïve desire to imitate nature was also true of the inhabitants of these rooms. While the seventeenth-century rulers might have chosen to withdraw into their studioli and contemplate their role within the universe that was miniaturized in the tiny objects that they collected, the mood now became outward-looking, with a desire to be at one with the natural world. The laws of nature, interpreted unquestioningly as morally good, were held up as an example for the construction of a human world-view.

Colour played a fundamental part in the new style of decoration, putting interiors in tune with the perceived light-heartedness of nature. Prescribed by French architectural theorists, fashionable new colours soon caught on. At the beginning of the eighteenth century decorative schemes had tended to be based on one solid, bright colour – such as red or green – for each room, accentuated by contrasting borders and trimmings on wall coverings and upholstery. By the 1730s, pastels, often used in a combination of colours, were preferred.

These are listed in surviving inventories under poetic names with natural associations. 'Aurorafarb', for example, according to Dr Johann Krünitz's widely used encyclopaedia of the time, was 'golden yellow with a gleam like the one that generally appears through the clouds shortly before sunrise'. Yellow in all guises, tones and shades – 'daffodil', 'lemon', 'straw' – was commonly used as a light background for carving and mouldings which were often painted silver, considered to be exceptionally noble because of its associations with the moon. Soft sky-blues, muted greens, greys and, for its brightness, pure white, were also popular.

The frivolity of the Rococo style coincided with the development of the idea of 'private' apartments at court,

The Music Room in the Altes Schloss at the Hermitage near Bayreuth (**left**), which was completed in 1737, and Schloss Mosikgau, near Dessau (**right**), which was built in 1754–6 probably after designs of von Knobelsdorff, are both unmistakably Rococo in decor. The Music Room, decorated for Margravine Wilhelmine of Bayreuth whose initials are carved into the marble mantelpiece, has graceful stucco mouldings set against gently marbled walls, while the pale blue of the ceiling is suggestive of the open sky. The paintings, by Antoine Pesne, of the Margravine's friends, lovers and rivals, take the place of what, in an earlier age, would have been ancestral portraits. At Schloss Mosikgau similar blue-grey colours are seen in the room that is reflected in the mirror, while in the foreground silver-gilded mouldings by Johann Michael Hoppenhaupt are set against a deep shade of one of the era's most popular pastel colours. In both rooms, the vogue for organic forms is seen in ornately carved furniture, especially the console table, which is almost an integral part of the wall mouldings.

33

Right The Amalienburg pleasure palace, designed by François Cuvilliés the Elder, in the grounds of Munich's Nymphenburg Palace, was built between 1734 and 1739 ostensibly as a hunting lodge, but it served as a private hideway where the stiff formality of court could be abandoned. French windows lead directly out on to the terrace; they let in as much light as possible – light that is then reflected by an abundant use of mirror glass inside.

Right The Amalienburg contains a showy kitchen covered in colourful Delft tiles that are composed to portray magnificent vases of flowers and ornamental columns. Chinoiserie designs on the ceiling and panelled surfaces complete the scene. No genuine kitchen activity actually took place here: it was only equipped to keep warm the food that was brought in from the main palace.

and the subsequent differentiation between state and private rooms. Solemn, prestigious interiors were, after the 1730s, restricted to state rooms – of which the most impressive examples are the ceremonial apartments, the 'Rich Rooms', in the Munich Residenz, designed by Cuvilliés in 1730–7. Meanwhile private rooms were taking on quite different functions, serving the purposes of *divertissement* and indulging flights of fancy. These roles were expressed most beautifully in the garden pavilions and summer houses in the parks of the royal residences; and the jewel among them all is the exquisite little Amalienburg palace in the gardens of Nymphenburg Palace outside Munich, designed by François Cuvilliés the Elder for the Bavarian Elector Carl Albrecht and his Habsburg consort Kurfürstin Maria Amalia.

It was the fourth *maison de plaisance* or 'Lustschlösschen' to be built at Nymphenburg. The elector's predecessor, Max Emanuel von Bayern, had already erected three, all designed by the Bavarian architect Johann Effner: the Pagodenburg, decorated with chinoiserie designs in 1716–19, the Badenburg, with a large indoor swimming pool in 1718–21, and the artificial ruin of the Magdalenenklause, which had a Gothic exterior and an interior in the form of a grotto, in 1725–8. However, the sheer brilliance as well as the consistency of the decoration of the Amalienburg puts all these earlier pavilions in the shade. The sumptuous carving, the stucco work and the use of colour and painted ornament take their inspiration from nature, and even the exterior ground plan is a captivating interplay of convex and concave curves that echo the living forms of the surrounding nature.

The interior of the small single-storey structure – it has only nine rooms – is laid out entirely to impress and surprise,

which was the *raison d'être* of this style of architecture. The *pièce de résistance* is the central hall of mirrors. Ceiling-height glazed doors let the light in on two sides and the simultaneous reflection of the trees in the surrounding park and the silver fronds of foliage which clothe the walls creates a deceptive intermingling of nature and architecture. The other rooms – one with niches in the walls for the beloved hunting dogs, a retiring room, a small boudoir, another room with representations of pheasants – point to the conception of this pavilion as a private hunting lodge. From its roof terrace, and with minimum effort, court society could shoot at pheasants in the surrounding reserve. Maria Amalia herself had a more robust attitude: she loved to hunt – and did so in men's clothing, adored her dogs and was a superb shot.

The presence of a large, wonderfully ornate kitchen with decoratively tiled walls is unusual. In most of the other park pavilions the kitchen was either in a special outbuilding or in the cellar, so that the aristocratic company could remain undisturbed. Large, grand kitchens, like those common in bourgeois homes, served less for the purposes of cooking than for the display of copper pots, brassware, faïence or other precious household items. It is likely that this was also the intention of the Amalienburg kitchen, for an inventory of 1751 describes the collection of faïence stored in the cupboards as 'not intended for use, but only for looking at'. Neither could the weighty pans on large tripods have been practical for cooking; and the hollows in the stoves for setting pots in hot water indicate that food was only ever warmed up here rather than being freshly cooked. Nannerl Mozart, the composer's sister, was obviously mistaken when she reported in a letter that 'Amalienburg is the most beautiful

The Amalienburg's hall of mirrors combines all the principles of Rococo ornament to full effect. There seems to be no boundary between this light-flooded room and its natural surroundings: the mirrors bring the outside world into the room which, with its light blue ceiling, seems itself to be open to the heavens. The fanciful natural imagery of the gilded stucco, crowded with nymphs, goddesses and dogs, provided an appropriately light-hearted setting for the festive hunting parties of the pleasure palace's first inhabitants.

Right The Sun Temple at the Hermitage was constructed between 1749 and 1753 based on Margravine Wilhelmine's own plans. It once formed the centrepiece of the colonnaded semicircle of buildings that made up the Neues Schloss, but unfortunately it was possible to re-create only the exteriors after damage incurred during the Second World War. Specific decorative materials were chosen to bring the temple as close to nature as possible. Its walls were originally encrusted with fragments of red, blue and yellow glass which when the sun shone must have produced the most unworldly effect, glinting through the mist from the fountains.

Right The close association with water throughout the Hermitage park is underlined by the grotto in the Altes Schloss, a building that the margravine created by vastly extending an existing one. Moss-covered pebbles and shells cover the walls and, with the Brandenburg eagle, form a background to aquatic images such as dolphins and mermaids.
Below The spartan hermit's quarters, from which the Hermitage park got its name, are the only remaining feature of the first building in the park. They were intended to be a place of retreat and stand in deliberate contrast to the otherwise exuberant presence of nature.

place, . . . and the Kurfürstin herself did the cooking in the little kitchen'. It was in just such affectation that court society took its pleasure: in the search for the imagined happiness of the simple life they performed a kind of masquerade, emulating the tasks of an everyday life amid a beautified version of nature.

A sentimental attitude to nature was revealed by the young Crown Prince of Prussia, later Friedrich II – known more commonly now as Frederick the Great – when he wrote to his favourite sister Wilhelmine in 1737, 'The country life means a thousand times more to me than city and court life. It is more natural, more comfortable, more honest and more informal.' Full of the melancholy that affected him all his life, he went on, 'But the truth is there is no point in pining away for the sake of a title when life is so short! Don't forget me in your enchanted garden and know that you can always rely on my tenderness, which will not cease until I die.' Wilhelmine's 'enchanted garden' was the Hermitage, one of the most beautiful Rococo ensembles of landscape design and imaginative architecture, set in the park outside the gates of the city of Bayreuth.

After the failure of her engagement to the heir to the British throne, later George II, Wilhelmine was forced to marry the Margrave of Bayreuth and live in what was then considered the provinces. There, in the Hermitage park, she created her own realm, unrivalled in its originality. She enlarged the small existing building, making what is known as the Altes Schloss and constructed another one, the Neues Schloss, and laid out fantastic gardens around these from 1736–44, filling them with smaller fanciful buildings. The park soon became famous: it features in the accounts of many eighteenth-century travellers, and the waterworks and fountains were described with awe by a character in a novel by Jean Paul in 1796.

The park was named after the existing building, which had been installed by the Margrave's predecessor Georg Wilhelm in 1715. Spartan hermit's quarters, furnished with little more than a bed, a chair and a table, have survived from the original construction, whose outer walls were clad in rough-hewn stone to give the effect of bare rock. The concept of a hermitage within a landscaped garden was not a new one; similar conceits already existed in France, including one built for Louis XIV at Marly near Versailles. In Bayreuth, however, the gardens were not laid out strictly symmetrically, with avenues radiating out from circular beds, as they were in France. Instead, its winding paths, which fit naturally into the landscape and provide frequent viewpoints, formed the first so-called English style landscape garden on German soil. In England Caroline, wife of George II,

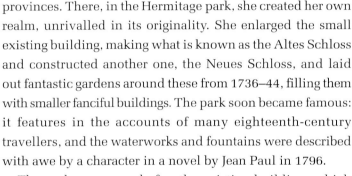

(who had been born a German princess at Ansbach) had included a Hermitage in the garden she laid out in Richmond, near London, in 1726. The original sense of the word hermitage as the domain of a solitary hermit played a far greater part in Bayreuth than in France, however, where hermitages had been stripped of all their spiritual connotations and instead were created as playful retreats from the stiff ceremony of court. In a letter to the French philosopher and writer Voltaire, who visited her in Bayreuth with her brother, Wilhelmine called herself the 'abbess', and invited Voltaire to visit her again in her 'convent'; and in her memoirs she portrayed herself with resignation as a hermit, for whom 'the hours of isolation are the sweetest', thus echoing the words of the man who had built the first hermitage there: 'Being alone brings me the greatest pleasure.'

In 1736 Wilhelmine altered the basic structure of the Altes Schloss, adding two wings, each with five ground-floor rooms, which she proceeded to decorate in her own idiosyncratic way over the next fifteen years. The most original room designs are found in the ladies' wing, where the Japanese Lacquer Room and the Chinese Cabinet of Broken Mirrors show how she adapted the contemporary fashion for chinoiserie to her own, highly personal, vision. In the Cabinet of Broken Mirrors, decorated in 1751, framed mirror fragments of varying sizes cover the walls so that the room appears, bizarrely, to be full of holes. The only truly Chinese feature is the scenes on the ceiling. Painted by wallpaper artists, these were taken from a series of widely distributed chinoiserie pattern books printed in Augsburg. In contrast to the magnificent German cabinets of mirrors of the late Baroque and early Rococo periods, such as that at Schloss Pommersfelden, whose reflecting walls create an illusion of endless depth to the delight of the astonished visitor, this cabinet of fragments with its ravaged air captures something of the lingering melancholy of its creator.

The Japanese Lacquer Room had been created a few years earlier. Frederick the Great had given his sister two original East Asian lacquer panels and, with the help of her court

The new European vogue for exotic ornament was employed by Margravine Wilhelmine to an effect that is endearingly naïve but also borders on the bizarre. It is illustrated here in the Japanese Lacquer Room, c. 1739 (**left**) and the Chinese Cabinet of Broken Mirrors, c. 1751 (**right above**) both in the Altes Schloss at the Hermitage, and in the 'Cabinet of Broken Mirrors', c. 1750 (**right below**) in the Neues Schloss in Bayreuth. The detail is almost overwhelming and the eccentric arrangement of mirror shards gives the rooms a disorientating air.

craftsmen, she built an eccentric 'chinois' salon around them. Just how close was the association at the time between exoticism and naturalism is illustrated by the bronze chandelier, decked with countless porcelain flowers, that was specially made for this room. Around the middle of the century there was a great vogue at the courts of the German aristocracy for sumptuous chandeliers and candelabra laden with exquisite reproductions of native flowers and plants. The factories of Meissen and Berlin competed with each other to produce the finest examples, and the label 'imitant la nature' was a sign that they were of the highest quality. A chandelier of this sort was bought for a garden room in the orangery of the nearby Seehof summer palace of the Bamberg prince-bishops in 1762. The room in which it hung had straw mats on the floor and furniture that seemed to consist entirely of painted vine-laden trellis. Sadly, it no longer exists; it must have been a fine example of the kind of naturalistic, so-called 'treillage' or garden-room decor that is also known as Franconian Rococo. The motifs that combined shells and stones to create grotto-like effects, which were so characteristic of the Rococo style elsewhere in Europe, had no place in the development of this increasingly distinctive German style.

The Neues Schloss in the grounds of the Hermitage was once a showpiece of this type of decoration. Built by Wilhelmine between 1749 and 1753, it was destroyed during the Second World War and, unfortunately, all that could be reconstructed was the colonnaded exterior with the façade of the Sun Temple at its centre. Earlier descriptions make the interior of the Neues Schloss sound quite fantastic: clouds were painted on the ceilings, and the walls of each room were covered in stucco trellis exuberantly clothed in stucco vines and foliage. In front of the walls stood artificial orange and lemon trees with twigs and leaves made of plaster, and with fruit carved in wood. To complete the illusion of an outdoor space, their branches were hung with cages with real birds, whose twittering combined with the sound of the gently splashing water that ran over a cleverly constructed waterfall of volcanic rocks. Little wonder that in her later years, which were overshadowed by disappointments and illness, the Margravine increasingly sought comfort here.

The city palace within Bayreuth was reserved for ceremonial use and though it offered little opportunity for individual designs, Wilhelmine was able to find a way to express her irrepressible creative instinct there too. Also named the Neues Schloss, this palace contains another Chinese Cabinet of Broken Mirrors and six rooms decorated in the style that had been used at the Hermitage: in some of these, the walls are divided up by gilded stucco latticework, in others with stucco tendrils; all are entwined with painted stucco plants and flowers. But strikingly true-to-life though the naturalism was, it had its limits: the cacti and cocoa plants reproduced in the 'Japanese' room, for example, would hardly be found as climbers in a real garden.

In the Palm Room in this Neues Schloss, the illusion of a whole palm grove has been conjured up in a long, panelled gallery. Originally the exotic impression was intensified by the presence of two ceramic stoves shaped like rocky outcrops on which lurked a lion and lioness, and console tables in the form of tree trunks that appeared to grow out of the floor between the windows. This room is so extraordinary

Right The desire to be surrounded with nature's idyll, indoors as well as out, inspired some of the most beautiful interiors of the German Rococo period. In one of the rooms in the Neues Schloss in Bayreuth, the naturalistic blooms which are threaded through the gilded stucco trellis panels and fronds on the walls are echoed in the carving of the pastel-coloured furniture. The upholstery fabric repeats the floral motifs as well as the pale background colour.

Right The Palm Room in the Neues Schloss in the city of Bayreuth, which dates from 1757, was one of the last rooms to be created by Margravine Wilhelmine. The wavy, flame-like grain of the walnut veneer has been used so skilfully by the cabinet-maker that it merges with the carved and gilded palm trunks, flowers and foliage that 'grow' up the walls. Gilded palm fronds stand proud of the vaulted ceiling, while golden stucco dragons cavort across the gentle sky-blue of the ceiling. The metalwork stove in the corner is not original to the room; it replaces one that was far more extraordinary.

Left There is a mixture of styles in the Garden Room of the Italian Building, a pavilion set in the garden of the Neues Schloss in the city of Bayreuth. The sinuously curved mouldings, the shell motifs and the floral themes are a reminder of Rococo ornament, yet the ceramic stove, with its restrained swags, laurel wreaths and antique portrait reliefs, looks forward to Neo-Classicism. The Italian Building, which was begun in 1759, was commissioned by Margrave Friedrich for his second wife Sophie, whom he married after the death of Wilhelmine. The architect was probably Carl Philipp Gontard, who later went to work for Friedrich II in Potsdam. In 1764 the pavilion was connected by the so-called 'bath wing' to the Neues Schloss, so is now part of the main complex of buildings.

Right As late as 1773 the style of a garden pavilion was still popular, and was chosen for the oval room in the bath wing of the Neues Schloss. Here guests would find themselves apparently beneath a trelliswork arbour of climbing roses, but would be reminded of the building's nominal function by the two marble fountains with their aquatic subjects of dolphins, shells and putti. Although both rooms were restored and re-painted in 1932, the colours are similar to the original ones.

that its creation has been the subject of much speculation. The connection with the stage scenery erected in the Bayreuth Opera House for the Italian opera which included similar palm groves is difficult to overlook, but the educated Margravine would also certainly have drawn on literary sources for the design of the room: she had a collection of engravings and books on comparable subjects, including a picture of a temple interior supposedly of the time of King Solomon, in her library.

Wilhelmine died in 1758 and soon after the death of her husband five years later many of the craftsmen who had been in their employ at Bayreuth, including the Italian stucco artists, the architect Carl von Gontard and the cabinet-maker brothers, the Spindlers, were lured away to Potsdam, to the court of her brother, Friedrich II, where their talents were to shine. Here, in its so-called 'friderican' form, German Rococo was to flower in a final, gorgeous flush at a time when Neo-Classicism had already taken hold in the other royal residences and great houses of Europe.

As early as 1746 the young King Friedrich had commissioned the architect Georg Wenzeslaus von Knobelsdorff to build the summer palace of Sanssouci, in the park of the same name, at Potsdam. The spirit of Sanssouci, its name meaning 'carefree', was one of gentle gaiety and optimism, – in complete contrast to the King's melancholia. The lines of verse moulded in gilded stucco relief above the door in the drawing room can be read as a motto for the whole enterprise: 'If the sun, in its dazzling return, should find us lingering here in discussions of poetry and love, in a premonition of a yet more beautiful day full of joy, allow us then a glimpse of the flowers and the rosy dawn.' In addition to a drawing room, study, music room, library and gallery, the relatively small, single-storey building principally accommodated guest rooms. These were for the King's clever, witty friends whom he liked to gather around him for conversation and musical evenings. The artist Adolph

von Menzel depicted these soirées in a series of famous mid-nineteenth-century paintings, basing them on contemporary descriptions including, and most notably, some by the King himself. In a spirit of relaxed formality, groups of men sit together; the French windows are opened wide on to the terrace, and the King's beloved greyhounds have been allowed to creep beneath the round table. Even in these circles, away from the ceremony of court, hierarchy was not abandoned and the King haughtily, and somewhat ungraciously, recorded how his friends 'stuffed themselves silly', adding that though they must suffer from 'a sleep addiction', he none the less managed 'to have fun at their expense'. But the architecture and decoration of Sanssouci are an embodiment of the King's sensitive side and his high ideals. The simple structure with generous French windows that lead directly on to the terrace and garden brought him in as close a contact with nature as possible – a feeling reinforced by the decorative motifs of birds, flowers and especially fruit which appear in gilded stucco, carved in

Left The Marble Hall at the palace of Sanssouci, which was begun in 1746, was the scene of Frederick the Great's famous round-table gatherings. Despite its majestic air and mighty columns, his love of nature is much in evidence. Floral motifs decorate the floor, and natural light floods in through tall French windows.

Right The fondness for natural forms is also illustrated by the furniture in the Little Gallery of Sanssouci: made by sculptors, the sofa seems to be constructed of branches and oak leaves. The scenes of open-air frolics in the paintings by Watteau, Laucret and Pater underline the original inspiration for Sanssouci as a pleasure palace in a vineyard.

the panelling, or inlaid in the marble floors; the function of the rooms – for music, as a library, and for guests – is indicative of his proclivities and interests; and by comparison to the grandeur of his official residence, the Neues Palais, the decor is simple and informal.

Friedrich was a man of conflicting personality and the same man who sent love letters to his sister's spaniel in the name of his own favourite dog was also a calculating, power-scheming, expansionist ruler. Having conquered Silesia, occupied Saxony and, in 1763, at the end of the Seven Years' War with Austria, annexed a part of Poland, he succeeded in making Prussia into a European superpower. Once peace was established, he embarked on a programme of refurbishing his palaces and building a new one, in keeping with his new status. However, although he had no lack of money to fund his projects, his problem was the scarcity of skilled craftsmen. Among the whole unsophisticated population of Prussia there was barely a soul with the artistic talent necessary to realize his visions.

So the King gathered craftsmen from other regions of Germany and offered foreign émigrés privileges and tax concessions as an incentive to resettle in the vicinity of his court at Potsdam. Since his father's time the 'Dutch Quarter' of the city had been home to émigré craftsmen from France and Holland, and now they were joined by stucco artists from Bayreuth, and the sculptor and bronze artist Johann Melchior Kambli from his native Switzerland.

In addition, numerous French silk weavers were encouraged to move to Germany. For a long time huge sums of money had been swallowed up by the import, chiefly from Lyons, of the French silk wall coverings that were *de rigueur* in grander houses. During Friedrich's reign, German factories were to put this situation to rights. Soon silk could be

The naturalistic decor of the palace of Sanssouci achieved a peak in the fourth guest room. Completed in *c.* 1752, it was already referred to in eighteenth-century inventories as the 'floral chamber'; even the chandelier has leaves of green-lacquered lead and exquisite white porcelain flowers. Set off by the sunny yellow lacquered panelling, the swathes of flowers and fruit, including melons, figs, grapes and pomegranates, that decorate the walls appear almost three-dimensional. Painted in striking colours and modelled in great detail, these favourite motifs of the King are joined by reliefs of exotic birds and animals – herons, parrots and small monkeys – which the artists would have encountered in the Berlin aviaries and menageries. The carving is by Johann Christian Hoppenhaupt the Younger, and the painting by Antoine Dubuisson. The silver-painted chairs, after designs by Johann August Nahl, replaced the original seating, which was also silver.

Details of the furniture and wall treatments from the Neues Palais at Potsdam, dating from different times, reveal how little the fundamental elements of the so-called friederican Rococo style changed during the twenty years that was spent on decorating the palace. The dominant motifs – stylized shells, bird wings, vines and plant tendrils, flowers and fruit – were all derived from nature. In different forms, and often gilded in gold or silver, these appeared in carving, panelling and furniture design. They also decorated damask wall hangings and upholstery. The taste for the exotic was generally less pronounced at Potsdam than at the Bayreuth court of Friedrich's sister, Margravine Wilhelmine.

ordered from Krefeld and velvet from Hamburg or Potsdam itself, while Augsburg became the principal source of printed cotton. Eventually the long-term political and economic goals that lay behind the steps taken to furnish the Prussian palaces were realized: the rise in internal trade stimulated both by the royal commissions and by the inspiring example of foreign craftsmen culminated, at the end of the century, in a flourishing new tradition of Berlin craftsmanship.

Friedrich had very strong views on taste. When he ordered a Meissen dinner service in 1762, for example, he demanded that 'the decoration should consist of beautiful flowers, such as roses, poppies and lovely primulas, skilfully painted in the correct proportions and with care taken to ensure that the colours do not clash'. And he had a deciding hand in every detail of the decoration and furnishings of his palaces – so much so that Johann August Nahl, his first director of ornament, a post that made him responsible for all the elements of a decorative scheme, from the details of the wall carvings to the construction of the floors, fled to the court of a less autocratic ruler in Hessen-Kassel. Nevertheless, it was under Nahl, who held the post from 1741 to 1746, that the friederican Rococo style, with its fantastical schemes and striking use of natural imagery, began to develop. Nahl was followed by Johann Michael Hoppenhaupt, and then his younger brother Johann Christian, from Merseburg, near Leipzig. The Hoppenhaupts were the most significant designers at the court of Potsdam and were responsible for the almost forty-year-long supremacy of friederican Rococo. The younger Hoppenhaupt followed the elder's published designs, ensuring the stylistic continuity that the King craved.

All the craftsmen involved – carvers, *ébénistes*, stucco artists, painters and bronze workers – had to submit to the overall concept of the director of ornament, who himself was directly answerable to the King. For this reason there are few records of designs by individual decorators, which now complicates efforts to attribute work to specific artists.

A common feature of all the interiors is the sculptural quality of the furniture. Particularly striking are the gilded or often silvered chairs which, with legs in organic shapes, seem barely to stand still and certainly don't appear to be suitable for sitting on. Chairs with legs that finished in exuberant scrolls – otherwise only encountered in Venetian furniture – and with broadly upholstered backs became the defining features of the friederican style. Designs for console tables entailed so much fragile openwork that in the end wood was abandoned for the stronger material of bronze. Countless suites of furniture were finished by an army of carvers, many of them from Franconia, which explains the similarities in style of these designs which were otherwise so uncommon in Germany. The outlines of the furniture often echo the carving on a specific section of wall, making it unthinkable to move pieces around and ensuring that each integrates neatly into the overall design.

The moulded ornament on secretaires, commodes or the grandfather clocks of which Friedrich was so fond became increasingly important. Executed in gilt or silver bronze, it sometimes smothered the main body of the piece like a weed, without heeding the marquetry in the veneer. These superb designs were produced by the workshop of the sculptor Johann Melchior Kambli, who in 1752 received royal

permission to open the first bronze factory in Prussia. The forms and motifs were modelled largely on fauna and flora, but cavorting among all the heron's wings, pomegranates, melons and rampant flower stems were countless cherubs.

The ornamental design of inlaid floors and wall panelling was predominantly of flowers: the neat little flower baskets of the 1720s and 30s were gradually replaced by ever more extravagant floral arrangements, and from the 1750s the design of the floor became increasingly significant in a room's overall decor. Whereas for years people had been happy to make do with simple floorboards, sometimes laid in geometric patterns, the arrival in the 1740s of French parquet flooring in the style of Versailles, where it had been used since the beginning of the century, offered new possibilities. The pre-prepared parquet tablets from the workshops of the *ébénistes* could be laid in the most intricate designs which, in concert with the furniture, the decoration of the walls and the stucco ceiling, raised a room to the level of a 'Gesamtkunstwerk' – a total environment designed as one concept.

There are some fine examples of this in the Neues Kammern and in the Neues Palais, both in the park of Sanssouci. In the Neues Palais there are five small rooms or 'cabinets' made by the Spindler brothers with inlaid walls and parquetry floors. Evoking the impression of flower-filled garden rooms, they illustrate the nature-adoring ideas of the royal patron at their most beautiful. Flowers also appear in the stucco ceilings, but there the principal motifs are images of gods and allegories of bucolic idylls: Apollo and Venus, Zephyr, Pomona and Bacchus inhabit this peaceful, mythical world that was so far removed from Prussian reality.

The colour schemes of the rooms in Sanssouci and in the Neues Palais are also light and cheerful. Friedrich loved green as the colour of nature and fertility, although he hated the hunting with which this colour was traditionally associated. The shades of green used in Sanssouci and later in the larger Neues Palais are distinct and yet delicate, and are described in the inventories with names like apple green, celadon green and sea green.

Friedrich had begun work on the plans for the Neues Palais, his last major building project, in 1763, at the end of the Seven Years' War. In this palace, which was huge in comparison to Sanssouci and in which the King only occupied an apartment in one wing, the naturalistic schemes of friderican Rococo reached a final climax. The decorative designs of Nahl and the Hoppenhaupts were reproduced in the finest materials – tortoise shell, silver, gold, jade and other semi-precious stones, and the walls were covered in the most opulent silks. Much of the intricate panelling and furniture was made from cedar wood, which – as a visiting English lady remarked in 1773 – continued to perfume the rooms for years afterwards.

Porcelain objects were also an important element in the decorative schemes. Friedrich had ordered most of his pieces from Meissen, the leading porcelain manufacturers, and records show that he commissioned over two hundred animal sculptures from there, chiefly different types of native and exotic birds, such as woodpeckers and parrots, which echoed the imagery of the stucco and inlay designs. He also bought examples of the popular Meissen pug dogs, prized as symbols of courage and loyalty, for commodes and other display surfaces. However, in 1763 he took over a small Berlin porcelain factory, after which it became known as the Konigliche-Porzellan-Manufaktur (KPM). It had had a patchy existence but, once Friedrich had personally taken it in hand and his palaces had become its chief customers, it began to flourish. The close association between the King and the factory explains why the same relief patterns appear both on the porcelain and in the room's mouldings – in trelliswork, vine tendrils, palm trunks and jagged stalactites, for example. Friedrich's personal taste is also reflected in the painting on the porcelain: as well as endless repetitions of the beloved flower arrangements, were designs taken from engravings of the King's favourite paintings by the French artists Boucher and Watteau.

Count Lehndorff, who spent some time in Paris in 1768, compared the decor of the palaces at Potsdam and Versailles: in his estimation they were barely distinguishable. What he did find baffling, however, were the extraordinarily opulent and fashionably furnished *hôtels* of the private residents of Paris. Such houses barely existed in Prussia. Limited to the narrow circles of the royal family, Rococo as it appeared in Potsdam was purely a court style, dictated by Friedrich's taste and therefore justifiably earning the name of 'friderican' Rococo. The style died with its royal patron in 1786.

As late as 1759 Voltaire had written mockingly of the culture of the general populace of Berlin, the capital of Prussia, reporting that lately 'some people have acquired furniture, and the majority even wear shirts'. Berlin had always been a garrison town, and street life was dominated by soldiers, who were so numerous that they had to be quartered in private houses. The best visual evidence of the living conditions and bourgeois interiors of the time are provided by the widely distributed etchings of Daniel Chodowiecki, an artist from Danzig who became famous in Berlin as a miniaturist and an illustrator. His prosaic portrayals of everyday life in scenes with titles such as *The Lying-in Parlour*, *The Sick Room*, or *At the Dressing Table* are the clearest evocations of life in the late-friderican period. A growing desire for more light

Left The extreme naturalism of the carved furniture which the Hoppenhaupts designed for Frederick the Great 's Neues Palais in the park of Sanssouci made it almost too fragile to be of practical use. However, in the eighteenth century the seating would have been used not for conversation in the way that is suggested by the arrangement of this group, but lined up against the wall and used only rarely, as part of the ceremonial life of court .

Opposite Meissen 'snowball vases', each displaying exquisite garlands of flowers, were commissioned especially for Frederick the Great 's apartments in the Neues Palais. The King was a man with highly discriminating taste and an eye for detail.

in bourgeois homes is reflected in the pale colours used on walls and on furniture, which was routinely painted in white or blue. Sometimes housewives would dabble in decorating their own furniture, painting it or adding paper cut-outs. Tiled stoves, which had been huge, became slimmer and were often glazed in pastel colours to add to the overall effect of brightness. English-style chairs were popular; these were purchased from 'English' chair-makers who were, in fact, usually locals who imported or copied them. Upholstered furniture was a rarity, and most sofas or chairs had rush seats. The new fashionably elaborate clothes could not be stored in trunks, but had to be hung in wardrobes so vast that they had be be placed on landings. The one expensive piece of furniture and the family's pride and joy was usually a tall secretaire.

The patronage of the wool and silk factories, the gold and silver workshops and the manufacture of porcelain may have resulted in a visible rise in trade in and around Berlin, but it was only after a hesitant start that there was any knock-on effect in the quality of furnishings in bourgeois homes. In the early years of Frederick the Great's reign, neither the nobility nor the bourgeoisie of this permanently war-torn kingdom could afford any expensive furniture or decoration. The creation of intricately carved furniture and other decorative objects was time-consuming and highly skilled, and therefore extremely costly, putting it effectively out of reach for most people. Ironically, the exclusivity with which the style was associated was to become one the reasons for its popularity when it was revived in the mid-nineteenth century, in the 'second wave' of Rococo, and again, towards the end of the century, in the 'third wave'.

Fashions from abroad were not as well known in the 1740s as they were to become a few decades later through the popular new newspapers and magazines. The general standard of

education among the population was low, with approximately eighty per cent being illiterate. Before 1770 intellectuals spoke French, which was also the language of the court, but hardly anybody could speak English. After the death of Frederick the Great in 1786 the population of Berlin consisted of 145,000 people, making it the second largest German town after Vienna. However, on all levels its cultural life was still a long way from being equal to that of other European capitals. In matters of taste the educated classes no longer took all their cues from the royal court. Classicism had already made an entrance with the ideas of the bourgeois Enlightenment and brought with it new attitudes to interior design which were eventually to bring about another flowering of German domestic culture.

The Classically inspired stove, sparse furnishings, simple wooden floor-boards and the latest fashion in wallpapers in Schiller's house (see pages 98–103) was typical of the interiors of the houses of the Weimar poets.

Neo-Classicism and the Biedermeier style

The impact of Classical antiquity and the taste of the new bourgeoisie in the late eighteenth and early nineteenth centuries

The excesses of the Rococo were almost bound to cause a reaction, and initially the imitation of Classical antiquity was a means to create a style that was more rational and noble than the Rococo. It was only towards the nineteenth century that it became an end in itself. The swing of the style pendulum coincided with, and became a manifestation of, a new intellectual mood that swept across Europe. Associated with the new, Neo-Classical, style – which was to alter people's outlook on life as much as it was to affect the interiors of their houses – were moral integrity and regeneration, and when it was adopted in Germany, Rococo came to be considered not just aesthetically, but also morally outdated. What we now know as the Biedermeier style, which followed in the wake of Neo-Classicism, could perhaps be considered a further extension of that mood: the values associated with it were essentially those of the bourgeois middle class – family, modesty and comfortable informality – and the antithesis of the aristocratic extravagances of the Rococo.

In Germany it was the great writers of the time who led the debates over the new style. As early as the late 1760s, when he was still a student, Goethe was railing against the 'curlicue' style. And by the 1790s, as vehemently as he ranted against the convoluted narratives and the tortuous arabesques in the poetry of his contemporary Jean Paul, he distanced himself from the over-ornate decorative schemes of the previous generation in his own novel of 1795, *Wilhelm Meisters Lehrjahre* (*Wilhelm Meister's Apprenticeship*). In this he has his hero ask of his dutiful mother, the very embodiment of decent, house-proud domesticity, 'These silk wall coverings, this English furniture, are they not all unnecessary clutter? Could we not make do with less? For I must confess I find these striped walls, these countless repetitions of flowers, curlicues, little baskets and figures most displeasing.' He wishes that all the unnecessary ornament could be whisked away like a piece of stage scenery

Left top Austere, yet comfortable, Schloss Tegel was designed by Schinkel in *c.* 1820 for Wilhelm von Humboldt. Here, among a judicious mix of both original and copies of Classical sculpture, sits a figure of von Humboldt's young daughter Adelheid as Psyche, by Alexander Rauch.
Left bottom Enthusiasm for the Classical world was boundless in the early nineteenth century. In the Roman Baths in the park of Sanssouci, designed by Schinkel in the style of a Classical villa and built during the 1830s for the Crown Prince of Prussia (later Friedrich Wilhelm IV), the sculptures are plaster-cast copies of the originals, but are displayed in the historically correct sequence of rooms, from impluvium to caldarium.

and that in its place he could look upon things 'which entertain, enlighten and elevate us'. In a description of his ideal room, he sums up the high expectations which people should have of their environment: 'All this elegance and beauty was expressed in the purest of architectural proportions, and everyone who entered the room seemed to be elevated to a higher plane as the effect of the art they encountered there showed them for the first time what it means to be human and what a man is capable of.'

This was symptomatic of a shift in the intellectual climate throughout Germany. Although the country had disintegrated into over three hundred individual states, new means of communication allowed for the rapid spread of news, theories and fashions into the corners of even the smallest principality. The first newspapers – known as 'intelligence papers' – were printed; diaries and annotated almanacs for housewives gave them tips on the latest housekeeping practices; dictionaries and encyclopedias broadened people's education; and popular novels influenced tastes and introduced new personal expectations. All this paved the way for new decorative ideas to spread into new social spheres.

The scholar Johann Joachim Winckelmann published his *Gedanken über die Nachahmung griechischer Werke in der Malerei und Bildhauerkunst* (*Thoughts on the Imitation of Greek Works of Art in Painting and Sculpture*) in 1759 and in 1764 in *Geschichte der Kunst und des Altertums* (*A History of Art and Antiquity*), he held up the 'noble simplicity and quiet grandeur' of the Classical world as a new ideal for art and architecture. However, for all the exhortations and noble ideals of the poets and intellectuals, it was to be another twenty-five years or so before their ideas were to materialize into a cohesive form of interior decor in Germany.

The fact is that there was a dearth of German inspiration after the flowering of native craftsmanship in the naturalistic schemes of the Rococo period. The members of the aristocracy looked abroad in matters of taste, and particularly to France

Right top When decorating his summer palace at Rosenau in 1814–17, the Duke of Coburg chose designs that included Gothic tracery. Influenced by the romantic spirit of the times, the search for a German national style and developments in England, Schinkel had by then already used Gothic elements in his architectural plans as an alternative to Classical forms.
Right bottom The furnishings and unshowy room decoration of the Biedermeier era reflect the value that was placed on modesty, domestic conviviality and musical pursuits. Weimar's Duchess Anna Amalia chose a similarly modest style for her country seat of Schloss Tiefurt, which dates from *c.* 1800.

— so much so that in 1798 Johann Adam Weiss, an economist from Frankfurt am Main, complained that 'The German craftsman's life is made still harder by the excessive import of foreign goods to satisfy the dictates of fashion, and by the shameful prejudice which can only find fault with German workmanship and sees beauty only in objects from abroad. How many of the unpatriotic noble and rich will not allow anything into their homes, and certainly will not buy any goods that do not bear the sacred label of Paris or London.' What Weiss overlooked was that much of what was being imported was in fact the work of emigré German craftsmen.

This was certainly true of a substantial majority of the *ébénistes* who were responsible for the most exquisite Louis-XVI furniture in Paris. The *ébéniste* workshops run by Abraham Roentgen and his son David, for example, became one of the most highly regarded in Europe. Their clients included not only the imperial court in Vienna, the German prince-bishoprics and the Prussian royal family, but also the courts of Versailles and of Catherine the Great in Russia. Two features made their work internationally sought-after. Their

marquetry — the designs often copied from paintings — was unequalled: delicate, colourful and durable; and many of their pieces were technical wonders, and contained musical automata or other impressive gadgets made by the most skilful of contemporary watchmakers and mechanics.

Although the furniture designs developed by the Roentgen workshops reflect the importance of Paris and London, they also show what German craftsmen were capable of when given the chance to work under optimum conditions. The family operated under the wing of a religious community whose far-flung trading relations, resulting from its missionary activity, enabled the Roentgens to acquire exotic wood veneers with relative ease and released them from the centuries-old restrictions of the guilds.

The earliest Neo-Classical building in Germany was the Hauptschloss (1769–73), the principal palace in the parkland of Dessau-Wörlitz. It was created by the architect Friedrich Wilhelm von Erdmannsdorff working for, and with the keen participation of, his patron, the enlightened Leopold Friedrich Franz of Anhalt-Dessau, a philanthropic prince who

The province of Prince Leopold Friedrich Franz of Anhalt-Dessau may not have amounted to a grand principality, but the 'Garden Kingdom' that he created at Wörlitz was to be a lasting memorial to himself and his architect.

The Hauptschloss, the principal palace at Wörlitz (**above left and centre**) was the first Neo-Classical building in Germany. It was built in the Palladian style and finished in 1773. Inside (**opposite**) there is visible evidence of the

transition from Rococo to Neo-Classical style. The exquisite furniture by David Roentgen in the Princess's boudoir reveals elements of late Rococo in the curving lines and marquetry ornament on the table, as well as the straight lines of Classicism, displayed by the chair legs. The chimneypiece, purchased from Piranesi in Rome in 1770 and composed of fragments of Antique sculpture with contemporary additions, is more purely Classical, as are the

motifs on the door, stucco and painted panels. The Pantheon at Wörlitz (**above right**) stands on the opposite side of the lake from the palace. Completed in 1767, it is an example of that strand of archaeological Classicism which, in keeping with the spirit of cultural enlightenment, inspired the reproduction of smaller versions of prominent Classical buildings. Conceived as a museum, it contains copies of Egyptian art works and Roman sculpture.

The interiors at Wörlitz constitute Germany's most important collection of rooms from the early Neo-Classical period. Many of the sculptures in the palace (**opposite top right**) and those in the Pantheon (**this page and opposite top left**), were purchased by Prince Leopold of Anhalt-Dessau in Rome in *c.* 1800. Identification of the figures is not always easy, since, as contemporaries remarked, it was quite common to find 'muses spruced up into goddesses' through restoration or additions. Much influenced by the style of Robert and James Adam, a light, delicate version of Neo-Classicism that swept through England in the mid-eighteenth century, the architect von Erdmannsdorff decorated many of the rooms of the Hauptschloss after images on Roman plaquettes. On display in the dining room (**opposite, bottom left and right**) is a large collection of Etruscan-style vases that the Prince acquired directly from Josiah Wedgwood; the English influence is also apparent in the mahogany dining chairs. The cast of Bacchus from the original by Sansovino, the marble fountain and the vine motifs of the stucco are all pointers to the function of this room.

saw himself as a benevolent ruler with a duty to contribute to the beautification of his land. On his many travels, in the company of von Erdmannsdorff, he had been deeply impressed by the Palladian-style country houses of England. These early eighteenth-century houses, which were influenced by the sixteenth-century Italian architect Palladio whose work was based on Classical Roman principles, were precursors of the Neo-Classical movement. The Neo-Classical style had evolved in England and France, nourished by the excavations at Pompeii and Herculaneum and the publication of the engravings by Piranesi of these newly discovered Classical cities. Dignified and restrained, and aiming for nobility and rationality, the style is distinguished by its use of simple geometric forms and ornament borrowed from the Antique, and its quiet colours. These characteristic features can all be seen in the decor and furniture of the palace and a Pantheon that the Prince built at Dessau-Wörlitz.

Prince Leopold was also greatly influenced by the romantic park architecture of England, and during the last twenty years of the century he created what has become known as the 'Garden Kingdom', complete with fanciful park buildings, in the parkland at Dessau-Wörlitz. Near the Pantheon is the Gothic House (which was not merely a folly, but was actually lived in and used to accommodate the prince's art collection). The building, designed by von Erdmannsdorff and continuously extended over a period of thirty years (1773–1813), has façades that are modelled on the Gothic church of Santa Maria dell'Orto in Venice and on the English Tudor style. Every detail, down to the wooden cover of the romantic well in the courtyard, is covered with tracery. Inside the house, the original inspiration behind the building – the charm of the Middle Ages, the era of chivalry and the monastic life – is most evident in the Knight's Hall. This has a ceiling made to resemble barrel vaulting and is equipped with a specially commissioned suite of furniture, while the Prince's collection of Swiss stained glass gives it the subdued light of a church. Prince Leopold hung his early German panel paintings here too, to remind him of his forefathers, and he would come to this hall to 'transport his spirit into the past'.

At that time 'Gothic' taste was still viewed by most people as negative and, more importantly, as undisciplined. Although Goethe had written a veritable hymn to the Gothic age, 'On the German Art of Building', after a visit to Strasburg Minster in 1772, he then distanced himself sharply from any medieval inspiration, and it was not until after 1800 that the mood changed imperceptibly. In the shadow of the Napoleonic Wars, a small circle of architects and writers began to view the artistic achievements of the past afresh in a patriotic light and endowed them with a new significance as monuments of a German history. However, Gothic features still continued to be largely ignored by the decorative arts, and the influence of examples such as the Gothic House in Wörlitz was to have only a latent effect in Germany until around 1830 when they became highly significant.

Left and right The Knight's Hall in the Gothic House in the park at Wörlitz contains an eclectic mix of styles: old cast-iron chimney plates and an extraordinarily heavy suite of Neo-Gothic oak furniture, made to order in Dessau and crowned with decorative finials, combine to form an ensemble which, in 1775, had no counterpart elsewhere in Germany. The stars on the ceiling, which are reflected in the pattern painted on the floor, the Swiss stained glass and the Mannerist frame around a painting from the old palace are reminders of the Middle Ages. But the semicircular fanlights above the doors and the obelisks that rest on the mantelpiece and on the door frame are distinctly Neo-Classical in inspiration.

Right Constructed like a theatre set almost entirely from *trompe-l'oeil*-painted wood, the little palace on Pfaueninsel (Peacock Island) was described in *c.* 1802, a few years after it was built, as looking like a dilapidated Roman villa. Now the impression it gives is more one of a romantic medieval ruin. The delicate cast-iron bridge that links the two imposing towers was added in 1807.

Left The 'Otaheit Cabinet' in one of the circular towers was decorated to look like a South Sea island hut set within a watery, exotic landscape. Seen through the 'windows' are various strangely situated Berlin palaces including the little Pfauen Schloss itself (seen to the left) among unfamiliar surroundings. The imagery of the idyllic suroundings, with fruit, flowers and birds, reflects the contemporary yearning for an uncorrupted life in harmony with nature.

The effect the Neo-Classical schemes at Wörlitz had on the tastes of the educated classes did not go unnoticed in the royal circles of Potsdam, and when Friedrich Wilhelm II succeeded to the Prussian throne in 1786, he summoned von Erdmannsdorff to Berlin to advise him. The architect's studies in England had given him an unrivalled familiarity with Classical rules of proportion as well as with picturesque effects, and equipped with this knowledge and a royal patron, he became the main protagonist of a romantic form of German Neo-Classicism, distinguished from the more academic style of the Berlin designers. An eloquent testimony to his skill is the Marble Palace on the shores of the Heiligen See near Potsdam (which was built for the King between 1787 and 1792 and, like the Wörlitz palaces, was also set within a landscaped garden) and, in sight of this same building, the little Pfauen Schloss on Pfaueninsel (Peacock Island).

On this island, an objective of royal boating trips, a small white-painted pavilion, made entirely of wood, was built between 1794 and 1797 with a rusticated façade. The building was conceived as a place of retreat for the melancholy King, and its decoration was heavily influenced by his mistress Countess Lichtenau, the daughter of a court trumpeter. In some respects it still has the character of a Rococo *maison de plaisance*, but most of the interior is designed along English-inspired Neo-Classical lines, evident in the wallpapers and the complex parquet floors, laid in a different geometric pattern in each room.

One room in particular stands out: the 'Otaheit Cabinet'. Situated in one of the circular towers, it was named after the South Sea island of Tahiti as it was depicted in the euphoric reports of the French seafarer Count Bougainville (after whom *Bougainvillea*, the tropical flowering climber is named). His descriptions of this paradise could well be a motto for the idyllic little Pfauen Schloss: '... everywhere there reigned hospitality, peace, a sweet joy and every sign of happiness.' The cabinet's painted canvas wall coverings lend it the air of a bamboo hut bedecked with palm fronds, and the *trompe-l'oeil* views reveal extraordinary combinations of the Potsdam lakes and exotic vegetation such as palm trees and pineapples. No doubt the reports in *Reise um die Welt* (*Journey Around the World*), published in 1778 by Georg Forster, the German companion of Captain Cook, were also an inspiration for this room. His enraptured descriptions and drawings from the South Seas caused such a stir in Prussia that whole schools of poets, among them the aged Klopstock, became determined to travel with Captain Cook to Tahiti in search of an imagined paradise. Romantic interpretations of the theme of noble savages on distant shores continued to feature in many an exotically inspired interior until the late nineteenth century.

Decorated after 1795, the Neo-Classical interiors of the wooden palace on Pfaueninsel have been preserved and are almost in their original condition. Of particular note are the wallpapers and the parquet flooring, laid in vividly different geometric patterns in each room. Some of the ceilings were painted with a *trompe-l'oeil* effect, the illusion being of a squared ceiling in the manner of the Roman Pantheon. The elegant mahogany furniture, the work of Johann Ephraim Eben, is also original to this building. Eben, who worked in a similar style to that of David Roentgen, did a lot of work for the Prussian court, especially at the Marble Palace at Potsdam.

Below The Tea Room is decorated in a purely Classical style, except for the colourful wallpaper border. The walls are hung with monochrome plaster reliefs, modelled on the Antique and set into frames, and a sculpture of the goddess Pomona with her two attendants, by the Berlin stove manufacturer Rohde, stands in the corner niche above the fireplace.

Opposite top left The First Conversation Room retains its original wall coverings of Indian chintz. The porcelain vases painted with views of special significance to the royal family are from the KPM factory in Berlin. This room was used as a bedroom by Queen Luise, wife of Friedrich III, when she was crown princess.

Opposite top right The pilasters which grace the walls are made from wood veneer rather than the usual marbled stucco.

Opposite bottom left Luise's lady-in-waiting occupied the First Cavalier's Chamber. The drawing depicts the Queen's marble sarcophagus which was designed by her husband with Schinkel and sculpted by Rauch. The wallpaper is the original, from the Christian factory of Berlin.

Opposite bottom right In another of the palace's circular rooms, the frames of the watercolours showing scenes from the Vatican museums were specially made to fit the curve of the walls. The light fitting is original.

Right The intricately laid parquet floor is the only clue to the royal inhabitant of this diminutive bedroom in the little palace on Pfaueninsel. It was deliberately furnished very simply, with just a camp bed and night table, for Friedrich Wilhelm III, and used only for short summer stays.

Left The original Berlin wallpaper with its flower and bird motifs is a reminder of the cheerful, summery nature of the surroundings. Wallpapers such as these, with their hand-printed borders, became increasingly popular in the years after 1800.

Meanwhile, the success of Napoleon's campaigns was forcing the German princes to make a decision either to align themselves with the Confederation of the Rhine on the side of France, or to take up the sword with other Continental powers such as Austria or Russia. The German state of Prussia declared war on France in 1806, which resulted in the French occupation of Berlin. At the other end of the spectrum, several parts of the old Holy Roman Empire, such as Bavaria and Württemburg, were elevated by the French emperor to the new status of kingdoms, while towns such as Frankfurt am Main stood partially under French protection. Thus there was a constant French presence throughout Germany in the early nineteenth century, whether static and billeted or on the march to further battles. The widespread adoption of French tastes was not surprising, but in fact was less because of any political allegiance or loyalty than, more simply, because Paris remained the uncontested epicentre of fashion.

Things were soon to change in Berlin, where the patronage of Queen Luise, wife of Friedrich Wilhelm III fostered a new and uniquely Prussian Neo-Classicism, seen principally in the work of the architect Karl Friedrich Schinkel. Educated by journeys to Italy and Paris, Schinkel was appointed to the Prussian Directorate of Buildings in 1810, and in the years that followed he designed the kingdom's most important buildings, giving Berlin its distinctive Neo-Classical structure. Along the avenue of Unter den Linden he built the Crown Prince's Palace, the Opera, the Neue Wache, the Architectural Academy and the Altes Museum. He was equally active in the design of furniture and interiors. Through his drawings published in *Vorbilder für Fabrikanten und Handwerker* (*Models for Manufacturers and Craftsmen*), which appeared in instalments from 1819, he created the formulae for a new style. Known as 'Schinkel-Stil', it soon became the style in which everyone with taste and education wanted to decorate their homes.

Left, top and bottom Built in Italian villa style with arcades and sunny yellow façades, this complex in the park of Sanssouci, loosely called the Roman Baths, incorporates the residence of the palace gardener and the tea pavilion. Constructed in 1829–44 after designs by Schinkel and Ludwig Persius, the buildings were inspired by the Crown Prince (later Friedrich Wilhelm IV)'s sentimental memories of an Italian journey, and were intended to have an exemplary effect on the villa style that was beginning to emerge in the environs of Potsdam at that time. Apart from the gardener's house, none of the buildings was actually intended for practical use: no one ever bathed in the Roman Baths, for instance. Instead, the picturesque setting served chiefly as a peaceful retreat.

One of Schinkel's most beautiful works is Schloss Tegel on the outskirts of Berlin. It was built between 1821 and 1824 for the academic and founder of Berlin University, Wilhelm von Humboldt. It is a jewel of German Neo-Classicism in which the architectural shell and the interior decoration are in perfect harmony. Inset in the exterior walls are casts of Classical statues and, inside the house, the rooms are laid out along Classical lines. According to von Humboldt's instructions the interior was to be

comfortable but also thought-provoking. In an exemplary manner Schinkel managed to combine the domestic needs of a Berlin family of the early 1800s with a display of the master's precious collection of Classical art. Rather than being laid out like a museum, a great many of the objects are integrated into the design of the rooms, with the effect that the patron's learned status finds immediate expression in the furnishing and design of his home.

This is apparent as soon as one steps into the cool, restrained entrance hall, which is shaped like the atrium of a house in ancient Rome. Von Humboldt wrote of this hall to his wife Caroline: 'It is beautiful to be greeted in one's

own house by the mighty gods. Ah! Life's only true moments of calm and greatness lie in the contemplation of their idea and image.'

At that time, around 1800, sculpture was considered the highest of all arts, because it illustrated the Classical values at their most tangible; and, because the first museums were only just being established, the home of an intellectual was the only place where one could encounter the sculpture of the ancient world – in the form of casts and copies. The acquisition of casts sparked off a real spirit of competition between Germany's great intellectuals who vied with each other as to which of them owned the better pieces, or whose house was the more beautiful. Von Humboldt was to write disparagingly of Goethe's house in Weimar: 'Only a few mediocre casts; I wouldn't swap any of our things for these.' In his own house in Tegel – which von Humbolt, incidentally, did not want to

Above Classical statues in niches on the outside walls of Schloss Tegel, in Berlin, make the leanings of the owner, Wilhelm von Humboldt, immediately apparent, while reliefs of the ancient wind gods on the corner towers, looking outwards in all directions, symbolize the open spirit of the house.

Right The entrance hall of Schloss Tegel exudes pure Classicism. The terracotta floor tiles, the plain Doric column and the sharply delineated squared ceiling were copied from ancient buildings and create a framework for the wall niches and reliefs as well as for the marble benches that Schinkel, the architect, designed. In the centre is the font of St Calixtus, which von Humboldt acquired from the church of San Calisto in Rome in 1809. A signature bears witness to the fact that the Pope himself approved its removal.

Left Von Humboldt's study in Schloss Tegel contains casts of several famous statues of Venus because he wanted to keep the image constantly in his sight. Like many other large sculptures in the house they stand on revolving pedestals, in order to be seen from various angles. **Right** It was von Humboldt's desire that his 'works of art . . . of whatever sort' should be integrated into 'the domestic life of the house', and the Blue Drawing Room is a fine example of a successful mix of bourgeois comfort with reminders of the noble art of the ancient world. Schinkel, the architect, loved this strikingly clear shade of blue and used it several times because of its clarity and association with the heavens. Though the house has been restored, it has been done strictly according to the original plans.

be called a 'Schloss', for the term carried connotations of princely grandeur and he felt himself to be a member of the intellectual, not the social, aristocracy – comfort and culture are combined. The entrance hall is the only room with a purely Classical character; in the drawing room and study the Classical friezes and sculptures complement the simple but elegant furniture with no artificiality, and almost all the rooms reveal a genuine domesticity with upholstered chairs and sofas, curtains, and functional desks and bookcases.

The only room whose function is out of the ordinary for an upper-middle-class dwelling is the Hall of Antiquities, on the first floor. Here von Humboldt's favourite sculptures are displayed on revolving pedestals against marbled walls of a delicate blue. Some are casts, but there are also contemporary sculptures by Thorvaldsen and exquisite columns of Numidian marble which, when he was ambassador, von Humboldt had once received as a gift from the pope. Schinkel furnished this 'marble room' sparingly, as befits a gallery. The only furniture consisted of two marble tables and, in the centre, a now absent circular sofa inviting one to sit in meditative contemplation.

In the stairwell, where there is no space for sculptural reliefs, Schinkel made skilful use of *trompe-l'oeil* effects. On the landing, for example, one of a low-relief roundel appears in the middle of a marbled panel. Two of his familiar candelabra – of which there were later to be many cast-iron reproductions – also appear there in *trompe-l'oeil*. The vaulted ceiling of the narrow passage that leads to the dining room is painted with his favourite theme of a star-studded midnight-blue sky, which first appeared in his set design of 1816 for Mozart's opera *The Magic Flute*.

Schloss Tegel is an example of German Neo-Classicism at its purest. It was built before Schinkel's journey to England in 1826 triggered a new affection for Gothic-inspired forms. It mirrors perfectly the opinions of its owner Wilhelm von Humboldt, who disapproved of the passion for the Middle Ages and was to speak out strongly against the medieval elements which later became the vogue in architecture and design. For von Humboldt, anything produced after the heyday of Classical antiquity in 'the only two beautiful countries on earth' was 'bound by the restrictions of necessity and duty' and therefore not a worthy model.

Left The Blue Drawing Room at Schloss Tegel leads into the Hall of Antiquities, which is laid out like a museum with casts of antique Greek and Roman sculptures on partially revolving pedestals. The decoration – the marbled panels, the detailed cornice and the ceiling area – is typical of the way that Schinkel reinterpreted Classicism. In the centre of the room there once stood a circular sofa designed by Schinkel, such as one would find in an art gallery.

Below The round marble table is one of two that were designed by Schinkel for this room. Standing next to the door is a huge cast of the Ludovician Juno, its monumental effect enhanced by the slanting light from the windows. In those days the original sculpture was one of the most highly prized works of Classical art; wealthy intellectuals competed to own a successful copy. Goethe too had a cast of the work in his house on Weimar's Frauenplan, but in von Humboldt's opinion his own version was far superior to the poet's. Glimpsed through the door is the Green Turret Chamber, once Caroline von Humboldt's drawing room.

Overleaf Schinkel skilfully gave Schloss Tegel's narrow stairwell the impression of space by dividing the walls into panels and painting them with Classical motifs as well as with candelabra of his own design in *trompe l'oeil*. Painted stars against a rich blue 'sky' was another of Schinkel's favourite schemes. Here it gives added interest to the vaulted ceiling of a narrow passage.

Another building of Schinkel's whose interior still conveys an authentic picture of the domestic culture of early nineteenth-century Berlin is the summer palace of Charlottenhof, remodelled for the Crown Prince – later King Friedrich Wilhelm IV of Prussia – in Sanssouci park between 1824 and 1826. The external appearance of this little single-storey palace, set within a carefully planned landscaped garden, is closely based on the engravings of Roman villas published by the French architects Charles Percier and Pierre

François Fontaine in 1809. The interior presents quite a different picture: each of the surprisingly few, modestly proportioned rooms is a perfect expression of Schinkel's own restrained – one might almost say bourgeois – variant of Neo-Classicism. Again, the starry sky makes an appearance here in the form of the star-studded blue skylight on the stairs leading from the basement to the rooms above.

According to the wishes of the Crown Prince and Princess, each room had its own particular decorative theme, based

Above and right Even in winter the west front of Charlottenhof, the former summer residence of the Prussian Crown Prince and Princess, looks as though it must be somewhere far further south in Europe than north Germany. (This impression is even more pronounced on the east façade, with its colonnaded portico and garden terrace.) With great skill Schinkel transformed what had been a modest German manor house into a Classical Roman villa. The griffins which support the stone benches were inspired by the arms of original seats sketched by Schinkel on his visit to the Roman sites of Pompeii and Herculaneum in 1824.

Right The double staircase in the entrance hall was modelled on the drawings of Roman interiors such as those published by the extremely successful architectural draughtsman Jean-Nicholas Durand as early as 1810. When it was first built in the early 1820s, the hall was plainer and more austere than it appears here, but it was embellished by Schinkel, at the request of King Friedrich Wilhelm IV, between 1839 and 1843. The elaborate parapets are cast from zinc, and the two circular marble reliefs by Thorvaldson symbolize midday and midnight. The table between them, with a sphinx pedestal, was designed by Schinkel, as was the bronze Nereid fountain made in 1843 by August Kiss.

on the use of colour, textiles and Classical motifs. In the long dining hall, where light floods in from the windows looking on to the garden, the scarlet fabric-lined corner niches and doors create structural axes for the overall design of the room. Schinkel borrowed the idea for the use of drapery in such dramatic Pompeian reds from the ancient wall paintings that had been revealed in the excavations at Rome, Stabia, Pompeii and Herculaneum. He invented and designed the gilded *papier-mâché* rosettes and clasps that support the drapery.

Textiles also played a prominent role in the royal couple's bedroom, in the tapered tent-like deep green canopy which hangs above their double bed. It was extremely rare for a royal couple to share a bedroom in the eighteenth century, and the fact that the Crown Prince and Princess did so is a testimony to their loving relationship.

Leading off the bedroom is Crown Princess Augusta's study. With its subtle colour scheme of pale pink walls, moss-green corded silk upholstery and silver-gilded woodwork, this room is a typical example of the way in which the architect's ideas influenced every detail. In his determination not to allow anything to mar his overall design, Schinkel even painted the lampshade for the desk himself. The silver-gilded desk is made of cast zinc and lead and had no precedence in the history of furniture. Despite its size, it has a surprisingly delicate appearance. It is complemented

by the Russian folding chair made of iron, which, being also a filigree design, again does not dominate the room. Friezes of Graeco-Roman dancers such as the one in this room, with its images copied from frescoes in Pompeii and from Raphael's *stanze* in the Vatican, enjoyed great popularity in the years around 1830, not only among the aristocracy. Reproduced in the form of printed wallpapers in Berlin, these designs allowed the noble-minded bourgeois family a chance to decorate their home in the style of the ancient world.

The room that used the most lavish amount of fabric is the Tented Room, beyond the main gallery, which served as a guest room. Tented rooms had already been in fashion for some time, but nowhere was the concept reproduced so faithfully as here. Back in 1790, when a similar room with blue and white hangings was planned for Friedrich Wilhelm II's Marble Palace in Potsdam, the style was still labelled 'Turkish', probably with reference to the close political links between the courts of Potsdam and that of the Turkish Sultan. Real tents in the Turkish style, such as those which were erected in summer on Pfaueninsel, are further evidence of the fondness of the Prussian court for all things oriental. The tented room at Charlottenhof, however, owes its origins to quite different influences, and the decorations for the Empress Josephine at Malmaison Palace near Paris must have played a very important role in its conception. There,

Previous pages With the addition of theatrical corner niches, Schinkel gave a symmetrical structure to Charlottenhof's central dining hall. Sculptures of Ganymede and David, representing the conquest of youth over age, stand before Pompeiian red drapery hanging from *papier-mâché* clasps. A rich profusion of fresh flowers always filled the special device, part-flower bowl and part-lamp, designed by Schinkel, that hung in this room which opens directly on to the garden through French windows.

Left The hangings and the elaborate trimmings of the bed of the Crown Prince and Princess are an exact replica of the originals. The Prince was extremely fond of this shade of green, which he also had on his study walls.
Right The subtle elegance of the decor at Charlottenhof is exemplified in the Crown Princess's study. Typical of Schinkel are the carved and silver-gilded palmette reliefs, which appear on the doors, the cornice and on the edges of wooden furniture. He invented the material with which they are made as an alternative to expensive ormolu bronze mouldings, which had to be imported from France. The silver-gilded lead and zinc desk that he designed, now protected by a modern perspex cover, was also an entirely new technical departure.

both the bedroom and the entrance hall were decked out with tent-like draperies in 1804, following designs by Percier and Fontaine. There was also a tented room in the little palace of Peterhof, near St Petersburg. The first one in Germany was created in 1790, after designs by Carl Gotthard Langhans, at the Marble Palace in Berlin (but no longer exists). Martial elements at Malmaison, such as poles shaped like lances to support the swathes of fabric, and folding iron furniture, evoked the atmosphere of a battle-field encampment. Not surprisingly, these had become fashionable all over Europe in these times of permanent war and turned up again in Charlottenhof.

A characteristic feature throughout this summer palace is the preference for native Prussian craftsmanship – no expensive French ormolu bronzes were used. Schinkel had already been praised by the Berlin press for designing every ornamental detail himself, even the patterns on printed silks. However, the verdict that 'Everybody rejoiced that they were Berlin stuffs and not Parisian work, and at how they surpassed the latter in taste, quality and elegance' was in fact politically rather than aesthetically inspired, and grounded in aversion towards an enemy nation whose emperor had just been defeated. And Schinkel was repeatedly criticized by his contemporaries for using inferior-quality materials, such as the gilded wood he used instead of ormolu on the elaborate table in Charlottenhof's central gallery. Nevertheless, his innovations, such as wood 'bronze' – a malleable confection of plaster, clay and sawdust that could be gilded – or his designs for cast-iron furniture, played an important role in bringing Berlin craftsmanship in line with modern production techniques. Although they might at first have been intended as an alternative to expensive foreign imports, Schinkel's new materials in turn gave rise to original design ideas. As such they are regarded as a fundamental component of Schinkel's contribution to the applied arts in modern Germany.

With its hangings of blue and white ticking, iron camp beds, folding chairs and striped wallpaper, the Tented Room at Charlottenhof was decorated in the early 1820s as a guest room, particularly for Alexander von Humboldt (brother of the Antique-loving Wilhelm who owned Schloss Tegel), a well-known naturalist and friend of the Crown Prince, and was intended to remind him of his journeys to the Orinoco river. When not in use as a guest room it was usually inhabited by the Crown Princess's ladies-in-waiting. To complete the illusion of a tent in the open air, the floor was originally covered with grass-green oilcloth printed with bunches of flowers. In its place today are simple wooden floorboards.

Two sets of rooms in the Duchy of Coburg, at Ehrenburg and Rosenau, provide important evidence of the developments in craftsmanship in the early nineteenth century. Ehrenburg, in the heart of the city of Coburg, was an old palace (see page 30) and soon after he succeeded to the Duchy of Coburg in 1806, Duke Ernst I began to think about modernizing it. Under Schinkel's influence the Duke decided to give it a Neo-Gothic exterior, but for the interior he drew on the Empire style in Parisian taste. This style was related to Neo-Classicism, but drew on specifically imperial motifs, such as laurel wreaths and eagles, as well as on those derived from ancient Egypt. However, the decoration of his summer palace of Rosenau, outside Coburg, was quite different, and

was to herald new, distinctly German, currents in domestic design during this period.

Ernst I had initially sided with Napoleon, but changed allegiance just in time to receive considerable reparations at the Vienna Congress in 1815. These sums of money enabled the Coburg duke – and many other German petty princes – to carry out extensive refurbishments of their residences. Ironically, the princes used the money chiefly to buy furniture, bronzes, silk and porcelain in Paris, in the very style of the newly defeated empire. However, since these were extremely expensive, they soon restricted themselves to buying single pieces from a suite of furniture, and employed their own joiners to reproduce the rest. In the

The little-known apartments in Schloss Ehrenburg in the Duchy of Coburg were decorated under the eye of Duke Ernst I in *c.* 1820. As an ensemble, they present a complex mixture of styles and origins and provide an outstanding example of domestic culture in Germany in the period around 1820. They are particularly important for their wealth of original fabrics, preserved largely because they have been so well protected from the ravaging effect of sunlight by heavy curtains. Not only are the fabrics rich and varied, but the sheer quantity of curtains, wall hangings and drapery reveals the important role that textiles played in the decor of the time; very few examples survive elsewhere. As well as much of the silk, a good deal of the furniture was imported from Paris, including the Empire-style suite of round table and seats upholstered in red silk seen opposite, bottom left, made by Jakob Desmalter in 1813. However, in order to save money, expensive originals were soon augmented by reproductions by local joiners.
Right top One of the original rich cut-velvet curtains shades a nineteenth-century bust.
Right bottom A Berlin porcelain vase dating from *c.* 1820–30 is painted with a scenic view that would have been well known at the time. It stands in front of the original silk wall covering in the Duchess of Coburg's study.

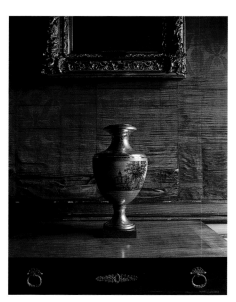

Opposite top left The Duchess Luise's bedroom at Ehrenburg was modelled on that of the Empress Josephine Bonaparte in the palace of Malmaison near Paris. Josephine's rounded, heavily swathed room was by Percier and Fontaine – who received their inspiration from Classical wall paintings – and had become very well known, and fashionable, through the wide publication of their designs.
Opposite top right The fashion of the 1820s demanded the inclusion of an 'Etruscan' cabinet in any house with any pretensions to being avant-garde. This style, using strong contrasts, had been made popular by Robert Adam in England in the late 1770s, and was derived from the decoration on Greek vases. Here satinwood (a light-coloured tropical wood) panelling has been combined with mahogany to a stunning effect. But in order to save some money on this lavishly decorated room, the palmette motifs were stencilled on to the veneer, not inlaid. The *torchère* of carved, painted, gilded and patinated wood probably came from Vienna in *c.* 1812.
Opposite bottom left The Duchess's study was named the Salon Cramoisi after the immensely costly original silk from Lyon that covers the walls and the upholstered furniture. The arrangement of furniture is an early example of the new, conversational circle.
Opposite bottom right The shelves of the Duke's reference library are concealed behind the original, pleated silk cupboard doors. The striking parquet floor reflects the designs on the ceiling of this semicircular room.

Left The laurel leaf motifs in the original lace curtains in the Duchess of Coburg's boudoir at Schloss Ehrenburg are echoed in the silk wall coverings.

Right Apart from the eye-catching, almost *trompe-l'oeil*, parquet floor, the scheme used in the boudoir (the bath in the niche was added in 1905) is one of the most gentle and harmonious interiors of German Neo-Classicism. The soft colours of the silk wall hangings are framed by the silver mouldings and pale blue-grey marbling.

palace of Ehrenburg these Parisian items of furniture were installed alongside German products such as tiled stoves from Berlin, and furnishings and candelabra from Vienna as well as Neo-Classical furniture from the Roentgen workshops.

The rooms in the summer palace of Rosenau, built between 1814 and 1817, are decorated in an altogether more autonomous style, independent of any French influence and more intimate in character. This palace, in which Prince Albert – later the husband of Queen Victoria – was born in 1819, is an intriguing combination of Gothic-inspired German historicism and what we now consider Biedermeier elements – most prominent in the black-lacquered furniture from Vienna, but also in the generally cosy atmosphere. The historicism at Rosenau is in fact largely restricted to the romantic evocations of Gothic tracery in the wall decorations, where quatrefoils and fleur-de-lys motifs are set off against bold background colours. Only in the latter part of the nineteenth century did architects, furniture-makers and decorators begin to strive for exact imitations of medieval ornament, in an attempt to recall what they regarded as the historical prime of the German people.

Duke Ernst I had visited Franzensburg, a Neo-Gothic garden palace built for the Kaiser in Laxenburg, south of Vienna, in the years following 1798. In decorating this palace the Kaiser had ruthlessly exploited the genuine medieval seats of his country's nobility, ordering the aristocratic families to hand over entire sections of their castles' interiors. This somewhat crude mixture of original features and Neo-Gothic designs, intended to re-create the environment of the Swiss Habsburgs, appears to have made an impression on the Duke of Coburg.

In Vienna the Duke also encountered the most important furniture-makers of the Biedermeier era, the firm of Danhauser. Founded by Jakob Danhauser in 1804 and continued by his son Josef, this factory stayed in business until 1838 producing original and creative designs that ranged from complete suites of furniture to individual pieces. It also published blueprints for decorative features that other joiners could copy and incorporate into their own constructions; these designs were distributed by means of illustrated pattern books throughout the length and breadth of the Austrian empire.

Much of the furniture and fittings at Rosenau came from Danhauser and from one other Viennese carpenter. The Duke had the chairs and sofas upholstered and covered on the spot, but with fabrics that also came from Vienna. At the time, Viennese textile factories were manufacturing the most imaginative furnishing fabrics, using daring combinations of colours in contrasting shades and tones. Often accentuated by borders and piping, these served to emphasize the character of the Biedermeier-style sofas and chairs which relied strongly on the fabric in which they were covered for their total effect. The most popular fabric was the printed 'Zitz', a kind of chintz with a dirt-resistant surface.

The fact that most of the work on the palace was carried out by local craftsmen of modest talent leads us to conclude that Rosenau's interior design is largely a product of the Duke's personal vision. The result is a harmonious ensemble of ornate parquet flooring, boldly coloured walls painted with Neo-Gothic designs, ebonized Biedermeier furniture and window drapery made from elaborately swagged muslin. The rooms have a distinctive air of informality that befits the palace's private character. Rosenau was formally opened in 1817 with a feast in medieval costume and a tournament, in faithful emulation of the Habsburgs, who had held similar celebrations at Franzensburg. Queen Victoria was enthralled by the atmosphere of the palace when she visited it much later with her Coburg consort Prince Albert, and she was to return on several occasions as a widow.

Above The intentionally romantically medieval appearance of the Duke of Coburg's nineteenth-century summer palace at Rosenau outside Coburg was accentuated by stepped gables and a crenellated tower.
Right The Duke's simply furnished bedroom fits a contemporary description of the design as combining 'princely splendour with rural simplicity'. While the gilded cornice and the dark, ebonized furniture show that he was still clearly influenced by Neo-Classicism in c. 1817, the painted wall decorations look forward to the revival of the Gothic style.

The most striking aspect of the interiors at Schloss Rosenau are the boldly coloured wallpapers and wall paintings in the English-influenced Neo-Gothic style. Although little of the original decoration survives, an accurate restoration of these rooms was made possible thanks to a series of watercolours from 1850 that have been preserved in Windsor Castle. The Gothic ornament is chiefly restricted to stylized elements of tracery and motifs such as the quatrefoil and fleur-de-lys, enlarged to decorate whole surfaces. It was not until the nineteenth century, when historicism truly came into force, that it became important to produce exact imitations of historical styles.

Opposite top left The Duchess of Coburg's bedroom was decorated in a hotchpotch of styles, with a starkly geometric floor, a French-influenced Neo-Classical bed, Gothic-inspired tracery motifs on the ceiling and romantic wall paintings of bindweed-entwined trellis poles.
Opposite top right The combination of Rococo trellis designs with an ornamental Gothic balustrade was unique to the period *c*. 1815 when Rosenau was first decorated. The trellis-work once framed what Queen Victoria described as 'the most beautiful views of Helvetia', painted on to the wallpaper.
Opposite bottom left Prince Albert, later husband of Queen Victoria, was christened

here, in the Marble Hall, or reception room, in 1819. The Viennese firm of Danhauser, which made some of the most celebrated furniture of the Biedermeier era, provided the chandeliers, made of bronze-lacquered wood in 'chivalric style' to complement the romanticized Gothic arches of the ceiling.
Opposite bottom right The black-lacquered chair, also produced by Danhauser, stands in front of printed, rather than painted, wallpaper.
Below Josef Danhauser invented this extremely popular type of sofa writing table with an integrated footstool. However, although this group of furniture came from Vienna in *c*. 1816, it was not actually made by him.

Whereas the princely interiors of the decade between 1800 and 1830 made full use of the international design repertoire, the members of the educated middle classes, unhampered by the nobility's need for pomp and circumstance, preferred to furnish their houses with simplicity and functionality. The outcome was often highly aesthetic, and in its later guise, labelled Biedermeier, came to have a profound and lasting influence on the history of interior decoration. This style of living can be seen at its best in the houses of Weimar's two literary giants, Johann Wolfgang Goethe and Friedrich Schiller. Even before the end of the nineteenth century the homes of these two poets had already become places of pilgrimage for devotees of German Neo-Classicism. As a result the interiors have been well preserved and – after some late-twentieth-century restoration and the removal of many dubious devotionals from the previous century – provide us with a true testimony to German domestic culture of the time.

Goethe's Garden House where, from the time he moved to Weimar in 1776 to his death in 1832, he would go to write poetry away from the stresses of the world, is proof of his theory that a comfortable and tastefully furnished environment, while it may lull one into a state of comfort, also induces passivity and elevates the mind. The sparing nature which distinguishes both this little house in the park by the River Ilm and the work rooms of his town house on the Frauenplan is the result of a deliberate scheme, which the poet was to sum up in 1829: 'Sumptuous buildings and rooms are for princes and the rich. Whoever lives there feels at ease; one is contented and wants for nothing. But that goes completely against my nature. In such an ostentatious dwelling I immediately become lazy and listless. A simple home on the other hand … like this meagre room where we are now, in a sort of ordered disarray, a little gypsy-like, is the right environment for me: it allows my spirit complete freedom to be busy and to create.'

One might be tempted to see the grand old poet's declaration as part of an elaborate self-deception, for the truth is that his house on the Frauenplan was thoroughly sumptuous, with reception rooms furnished with the singular purpose of impressing the ladies who came to tea as well as all his other numerous learned and noble visitors. There is nevertheless an almost spartan simplicity to the work rooms, both in the house on the Frauenplan and in the Garden House. Goethe had an aversion to carpets, believing that they often 'embarrassed' the other furnishings

Situated on a slight rise in the romantic park by the River Ilm which Goethe himself helped to landscape, stands his Garden House, a lifelong refuge for the great poet. He lived here permanently until 1782 and then returned to it again and again. It was in these peaceful surroundings that he worked on such famous poems as *Faust*, and this was also the scene of his early assignations with Christiane Vulpius, when he still wanted to keep his love for her a secret from Weimar court society. (He finally married her in 1806.) **Right** The Garden House contains just the few books Goethe needed to have to hand; his main collection of art works and learned books was kept at his more formal house on the Frauenplan in Weimar.

Opposite top Goethe set great store by the appearance of his external environment, and he himself designed the pebble mosaic which surrounded the house from 1830. The trellis-work for the vines and fruit trees that cover the walls became very familiar during the nineteenth century from the countless reproductions of the Garden House that were produced to satisfy the cult of Goethe worship. **Opposite bottom** The rooms of the Garden House were decorated and furnished with an almost stark simplicity, so as not to distract the poet from his work.

with their overpowering designs. So there were no carpets on the plain wooden floorboards, just as there were no curtains at the windows. The poet employed local Weimar joiners to make simple wooden chairs, glass-fronted specimen cabinets and functional desks, 'without excess fuss or frills'. He made do with a simple camp bed with cross-straps and a straw mattress. Throughout his house there was not a single Rococo flourish, no ornamental columns or capitals, no lions' feet or bronze mounts, in fact nothing from the vocabulary of ornament which was otherwise current at the turn of the nineteenth century.

As far as the decoration of the walls was concerned, there is evidence that the poet did not stick to his first choice of colours which had been governed by the rigid categorizations set out in his *Theory of Colour* of 1810. He began by painting his garden house in a cool green throughout, only to redecorate later with a strong yellow set off by red ceilings. The subject of colours, their inherent significance and their effect on the human body and spirit, was one of the greatest issues of the time. Even such a complex philosopher as Kant wrote an article on the subject in the *Zeitung für die elegante Welt* (*Newspaper for the Elegant World*) in 1804. Entitled 'On the Meaning of Colours',

the piece endowed each colour with a specific virtue: for example, yellow for candidness, green for friendliness or dark blue for steadfastness. In the sixth section of his *Theory of Colour* Goethe had argued for a 'sensual and moral effect of colours'. He recommended green wallpapers for rooms in which one spent a lot of time, whereas 'rooms papered purely in blue may appear larger, but in fact come across as empty and cold'. But the poet hardly practised what he preached: his bedroom in town changed from pistachio green to rose pink with grey-blue borders, only to be painted over again in apple green with a pink ceiling. Goethe loved nothing better than to rearrange his rooms. One reason for this was his ever-growing collection of art works – ranging from ancient Egyptian sculptures of Isis to contemporary oil paintings – which he always liked to display against an appropriate background.

The subject of the choice of wall colours and wallpapers, which had recently come into fashion, was also of the utmost importance to Goethe's fellow writer and rival Friedrich Schiller. Schiller had not been able to afford to buy a house in Weimar until 1802 when he bought the property of the English translator of his works, Charles Mellish of Blyth. Schiller lived in this house until his death in 1805; it was

In the course of the nineteenth century Goethe's Garden House was transformed into a place of literary pilgrimage and became crammed with a growing abundance of sometimes dubious memorabilia. Today the rooms have been returned to their former simplicity, a move of which the master himself would surely have approved. The floorboards are bare, as they were in his day; simple muslin drapes dress the windows, and almost the only elaborations are the painted skirtings.

Left The same simple, pale colour scheme has been used in all the rooms on the first floor.

Right above The elegant late-eighteenth-century roll-top desk against the window was used by Goethe. The three-legged chair appears in a painting of 1834 in which Goethe is shown dictating to a secretary who sits in it.

Right below The strange-looking half-height stool, which once stood at a high desk belonging to Goethe, appeared in a Weimar magazine as early as 1786. It is a practical, orthopaedic design that supported the spine when the user straddled it and rested his back against the hump.

It proved invaluable to Goethe during his long hours of writing. The upholstered settle, of a type that was particularly popular in Weimar, dates from 1790.

here that he wrote *William Tell*, and here that he would often meet Goethe, whose house on the Frauenplan was not far away. Although Schiller continued to live in constrained financial circumstances, he invested considerable sums, as well as a great deal of time and effort, on the furnishings and decor of his house, making them suit his own lifestyle, and that of his wife Charlotte von Lengefeld. The house was divided, floor by floor, into separate areas for domestic chores, for family life with the children and for his own, almost ceaseless work. On the ground floor lay such rooms as the kitchen and pantry as well as a room for the obligatory servant who, in the Schillers' case, was also on hand as a scribe for the master. The first floor was occupied by Charlotte and the children, while Schiller himself used the attic. Here, in addition to his work room, he also had his own bedroom, tucked away behind a concealed door.

The two men of letters were intimately bound up with the smallest details of the decoration of their houses. It is not known whether their two wives were granted a say in the matter. At one point they became engaged in a highly involved correspondence on the question of colours for the Schillers' wallpaper. Schiller's favourite colour for borders, which he called 'decorations on my horizon' was pink. The wallpaper in his study was spotted green, and it is rumoured that Goethe procured it for him and in so doing was responsible for Schiller's untimely death; for the green dye of the paper was arsenic-based and therefore poisonous. But this was true of all green dyes, the now infamous 'Schweinfurth greens' of that time. Since green was one of the ultra-fashionable colours, the discovery by a wallpaper

manufacturer from Schweinfurth of the first green pigment that would not fade in the light was greeted with great enthusiasm and the colour was used for all manner of decorative items. The legend of Goethe's treachery has long since been disproved, since the wallpapers he procured were in fact ordered for a different house.

The enduring charm of Schiller's house lies in the beauty and variety of the various patterned wallpapers with their contrasting borders. The triumphant arrival from England of wallpaper in rolls had recently replaced the earlier fashion for wall coverings of painted wax cloth. The general practice initially was to order rolls of paper in a single colour which were then fixed to linen backings and combined with hand-printed patterned borders. An article in the Weimar *Journal des Luxus und der Moden (Journal of Luxury and Fashion)* of 1787 advised against the use of patterned papers for large surfaces. According to the journal, not only would these detract from the engravings that were so popular in Neo-Classical interiors, but also the eye would become tired of seeing the same figures and ornaments repeated over and over again. Instead the suggestion was that the walls be divided into panels, edged at the top and bottom with decorative borders. The engravings could then be seen to full advantage against a 'soft' background colour. Skirtings and door and window frames should be painted a silver-grey – as indeed is still the practice in many Weimar houses. Another recommendation in keeping with the Classical look was for wallpapers with a marble effect. Tastes were, however, soon to change. Technical advances brought with them an endless variety of multi-coloured patterns, of

Left and above In the drawing room on the top floor of his house, Schiller kept a cast of the bust which his lifelong friend, the Württemburg sculptor Johann Heinrich Dannecker, made of him in 1794. This famous bust, different versions of which were to make Schiller's portrait familiar throughout Germany, was not the result of self-worship: the bestowing of busts as gifts to relatives and friends was part of the sentimental cult of friendship and memorabilia that flourished at the turn of the century. Goethe, too, possessed busts of fellow poets and philosophers, which, together with his copies of Antique sculptures, formed an integral part of his domestic furnishings.

Overleaf The family rooms on the first floor were decorated with wallpapers in designs as striking as those in the poet's private attic quarters. The squared wallpaper in Charlotte's bedroom was designed to look like cloth drapery, and their daughter's bedroom in the passageway was hung with a geometric-patterned blue-and-white paper. Built-in cupboards were disguised by jib doors covered by wallpaper, giving the relatively small rooms a sense of unity.

which the favourites were the time-honoured flower motifs and also imitations of drapery. Publications such as Friedrich August Leo's *Ideen zu Zimmerverzierungen* (*Ideas for Room Decorations*) of 1795–1800 led to a veritable boom in the use of wallpaper in domestic schemes.

What the interiors of the two poets' houses had in common with those of the bourgeoisie in general was an increasingly functional approach to furnishing and decoration. In the period immediately after 1800 this was to unfold into a new style, known later as 'Biedermeier' and regarded today as the quintessence of middle-class German domestic culture. Whereas Neo-Classicism was characterized throughout Europe by its interpretation of the Antique, and its stylistic

features were copied from the numerous engravings of much-publicized excavations, the designers of the Biedermeier age invented an entirely new language of forms and motifs. These were directed at a new class of patron, the bourgeoisie, whose domestic proclivities were for the first time beginning to dictate style. Germany's aristocratic families, whose roles were becoming increasingly bound up with constitutional issues, began to adopt these new styles in their residences too, at least in the private rooms. Family life was cherished as never before and a new spirit of domesticity grew up among both the bourgeoisie and the nobility.

The name 'Biedermeier' did not appear until 1855, when it was used in reference to a literary character. Herr

Left The Weimar poets, chief among whom was Goethe, often gathered at the Duchess of Weimar's little palace, the Schloss Tiefurt, in Ilmtal, during the summer. With the energetic participation of the young Duke, they spent the time playing pranks and publishing a newspaper. The Duke, a poet himself, took a keen interest in the original decoration of the rooms in 1779. Typical of the contrived rural look are the plain wooden floorboards, laid at a time when parquet flooring was *de rigueur* in most aristocratic homes. Refurbished in 1828, the rooms are a harmonious mixture of Classical and Biedermeier influences: the sofas and chairs upholstered in horsehair and plain fabrics; the simple grey-painted door frames – typical of Wiemar – and the panels in contrasting colours which were hand-painted on paper pasted on to the canvas backing that was battened on the walls.

Right In the period after 1800 there was an increasing similarity between the interiors of the homes of the aristocracy and those of the bourgeoisie. Schiller could praise Schloss Tiefurt as being 'furnished in a thoroughly simple and pleasing rural style', knowing that the same taste for simple, Classical-style furniture and bare wooden floorboards prevailed in his own home. The *vitrine* on the right – a display cupboard with glass on three sides – was an invention of the Biedermeier age, an outcome of a new passion for collecting, as well as a means to display porcelain to good effect. The stove dates from later in the nineteenth century.

Biedermaier [*sic*], in whose fictitious name a series of naïve, comical poems was published in a Munich newspaper, was intended by his authors to represent the typical German citizen, whose chief interests lay in a comfortable home, his family and good, honest home cooking, rather than in taking an active role in the politics of his day. But what began as an intellectual critique soon developed into a new model for living. Without anyone having been familiar with the term at the time, the period from about 1815 to 1848 was viewed nostalgically from the latter half of the century as the supposedly blissful 'Biedermeier' era. Not that the years in question were in the least bit idyllic, buffeted as they were by the struggles of a newly industrialized society compounded by the political process of unification. None the less the period saw a new style evolving in the urban centres of Vienna, Munich and Berlin which was to be among the most beautiful that German domestic culture has generated.

'Biedermeier' became synonymous with the furniture designs, fabric patterns and drapery favoured by the bourgeoisie of those decades. The classification had become so widely received by the turn of the twentieth century that a reassessment of the original elements was to sow the seeds of a Biedermeier revival that would come to embody the classical elegance of wealthy middle-class living. The term became absorbed into foreign languages and from that point on signified a typically German style. The values associated

with it were friendship, family, modesty and a comfortable informality. These were reflected in the forms and functions of the new furniture, and especially in the invention of what we now recognize as the classic seating group that formed the hub of the bourgeois drawing room. Here, an entirely new piece of furniture, a table, was introduced in front of, and to complement, the generously upholstered sofas that were so popular. Sofas, on which the lady of the house would sit to receive guests, were generally positioned with their straight backs against a wall. Equally well-upholstered side chairs (arm chairs were rarer, being heavier and more cumbersome to move around), often covered in a hardwearing horsehair fabric, completed the circle for domestic gatherings.

Display cabinets, either as *vitrines* with glass on three sides and some with mirrored backs for an enhanced effect, or as *étagères,* freestanding sets of shelves, were conceived specifically for the new cult of friendship and sentiment, with all the attendant knick-knacks, such as precious cups, beaded embroidery and silhouette cut-outs. Essential equipment for the industrious housewife – such as covered boxes and sewing tables – was often lovingly embellished at home, and printed with intricate techniques, or painted with indigenous flower patterns.

The porcelain factories of Vienna and Berlin competed with each other to produce ever more perfect representations of flowers on dinner and tea services, painted by highly qualified artists schooled at the botanical classes of the academies. Countless watercolours appeared portraying, with the same love of detail, the contents of individual interiors in order to evoke memories of home, which itself acquired a new set of values as the centre of the private sphere.

The secretaire was another key item of furniture in the drawing room. Most were similar in form: above two or three drawers for storage was a fall-front that made a writing surface, above which was often another drawer. Behind the fall-front was an intricately designed interior of small

Left and right Known today as the Goethe Room, after the poet who was a frequent guest here, this room and its lobby in the Schloss Tiefurt, Duchess Anna Amalia's summer palace, was originally called the Reed Room after the botanical decorations painted on the yellow linen wall covering in *c.* 1799. The painted oilcloth covering the floorboards, economical as well as suitable for a summer house, dates from the refurbishment of 1828. The symmetrical hanging of silhouettes, engravings and lithographs was inspired by similar displays in Goethe's house. The ensemble of sofa, sofa table and two upholstered side chairs, ready for conversation, is quintessentially Biedermeier.

drawers and pigeonholes. Whole teaching years at the Vienna School of Design for Cabinet-makers were given over to complicated construction plans for these, with secret compartments and hidden drawers. In fact, owing to an imperial decree of 1775 obliging cabinet-makers to pass an exam at the Academy of Fine Arts, the Viennese became the leading furniture-makers of the Biedermeier era, producing the most creative and original designs in this quintessentially German style. Although they had royal and noble patrons, their chief market was the increasingly wealthy bourgeoisie.

The economic misery which prevailed after the Wars of Liberation (1813–15) made it virtually impossible to import expensive materials such as French gilded bronzes or exotic veneers. So the cabinet-makers developed a preference for native woods, such as cherry, and for the bronzed wooden ornaments which were already being produced in quantity by workshops in Vienna. This avoidance of lavish decorative elements, initially due to force of circumstance, was soon to develop into the distinguishing feature of the Biedermeier style. The cabinet-makers discovered the fascinating effects that could be achieved with grains which, when entire surfaces were covered in a vertical veneer, gave the furniture its distinctive appeal. The fittings, whether on the individual drawers of a commode or on a cupboard door, became smaller and smaller, until eventually all that was left were the brass lock surrounds, leaving the full effect of the wood veneer to be admired.

The fabrics used to cover upholstered chairs and sofas were often strong in colour and yet abstract in pattern; this lent a calm, unifying effect to even large groups of the most varied forms of seating. The boldness of the original fabrics stands in glaring contrast to the restrained, scattered-flower

patterns which today pass mistakenly for typical Biedermeier designs. At the same time there was a new fashion for carpets, manufactured principally in the Austrian town of Linz, with similarly bold geometric or flower patterns. Among all this busy design and bright colours, plain white muslin window drapery, usually festooned and fringed, often provided the only point of respite for the eyes.

It was not long before a new set of historical references began to mingle with this clean and simple style, whose best creations look modern enough almost to be confused with Art Deco furniture of the twentieth century. The ever-present romantic influence of Neo-Gothic reappeared in the form of chair backs carved with tracery and secretaires topped with finials; oriental elements flooded in; and then the Renaissance became a new source of inspiration. Already in 1830 furniture firms in Munich or Mainz, such as Fortner, Pössenbacher or Kimbel, were offering the same models in a variety of interchangeable styles, and by 1848 the Biedermeier era was well and truly over.

Left After a long reign Duchess Anna Amalia retired to the Wittumspalais, next to the theatre in Weimar, in order to dedicate herself to intellectual pursuits. The palace was built and first decorated in 1767 after designs by Adam Oeser, who had taught the young Goethe design during his student years in Leipzig. Oeser himself was never a proponent of the Rococo style, and the restraint of his designs could be said to be an early form of Neo-Classicism. The watercolour above the late-eighteenth-century secretaire in the Green Salon shows a volcanic eruption – an example of the forces of nature which so fascinated early nineteenth-century society.
Right The Round Table Room was the scene of the social gatherings to which the clever, vivacious Duchess would invite Weimar's great thinkers. Wieland and Goethe, Schiller and Herder all sat on these chairs, as recorded in a painting of 1795 by Melchior Kraus. Here they would dine, discuss poetry or the latest theatrical events, or simply read Shakespeare.

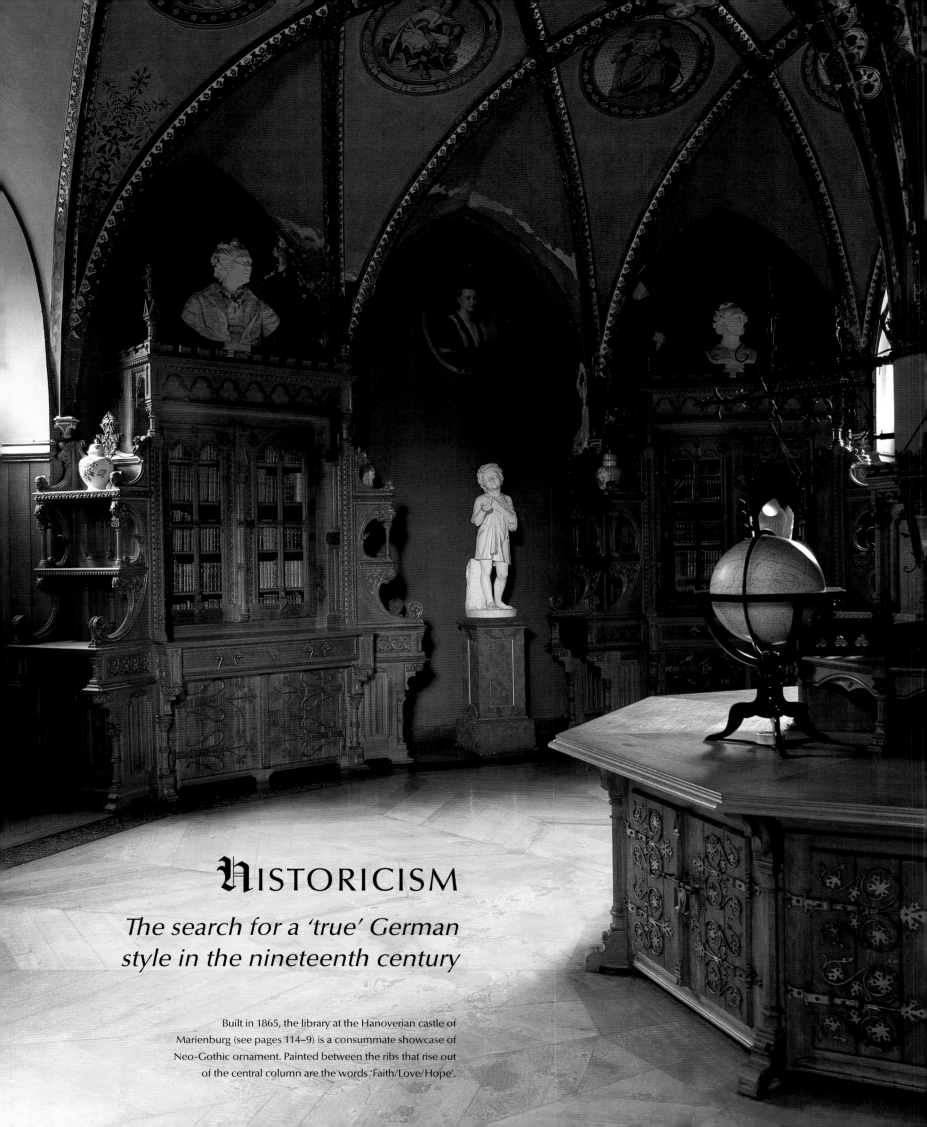

ḨISTORICISM

The search for a 'true' German style in the nineteenth century

Built in 1865, the library at the Hanoverian castle of
Marienburg (see pages 114–9) is a consummate showcase of
Neo-Gothic ornament. Painted between the ribs that rise out
of the central column are the words 'Faith/Love/Hope'.

Built between 1859 and 1867, the castle of Marienburg is one of the most important examples of German historicist architecture. **Left and right** The view of the north wing and the inner court reveals the eclectic mix of styles in which it was built: wide Romanesque arches, pointed Gothic arches and fanciful medieval castellations.

Opposite The starry, vaulted ceiling of the staircase tower was painted to resemble a medieval cathedral, the impression heightened by the quatrefoil tracery of the windows. The flags from the battles of Waterloo (1815) and Langensalza (1866) serve as a reminder of the peaks and troughs of the military adventures of the Hanoverian troops.

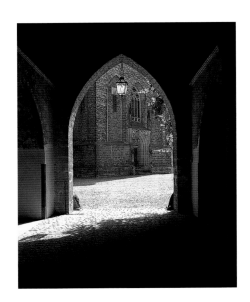

Few authentic interiors in this medieval style have survived intact. One of the finest is the castle of Marienburg, near Hanover, a present from George V of Hanover to his wife Queen Marie, as a summer residence. It survived unscathed the Prussian confiscations following Hanover's alliance with Austria in the 1866 war because it was the personal property of the Queen, but once she had been forced to follow her husband into exile in Vienna in 1867, it was never permanently occupied again. The castle is still in the possession of a member of the family, His Royal Highness Prince Ernst August von Hanover; the interiors are virtually untouched and present a superb, and unique, picture of German Neo-Gothic decor.

Queen Marie had free rein to design the castle entirely according to her personal taste. Both of the architects that she engaged – Conrad Wilhelm Hase from 1857 until 1864, and then Edwin Oppler – shared her fervent admiration of the Neo-Gothic style; indeed, all three were dogmatic proponents of it. No anachronistic materials were to be used in the decoration or furnishings of the interior; and every element in the construction of the architectural shell and the furniture was to be 'authentic'. In other words machine-made artefacts were deliberately ignored in preference to the perceived superiority of hand work. As work progressed, however, financial restrictions made it impossible to stick to this brief, and though plaster and cast iron were deemed unworthy, they were none the less used. The delicate, freestanding spiral staircase in the cloister is an undoubted masterpiece of technical achievement, but the fact that it was made from machine-made cast iron and not traditional

wrought iron detracted from its perceived beauty. Several cast-iron arches, which in reality did not need support, were given cast-iron columns to make them appear as though they were made of weaker wrought iron. Even most of the ceilings were, at first, not genuine: seemingly made of wood and lined with Gothic ribbing, they were in fact moulded from stucco and painted to look like wood. Only on the Queen's insistence were many of them rebuilt in oak. The hot-air central-heating system was augmented and made to seem irrelevant by the magnificent open fireplaces which are the centre of attention in almost every room. Designed by Oppler, they combine Romanesque and Gothic decorative features, as well as some sinuous flowing curves that would become part of the Jugendstil vocabulary a few decades later.

The most beautiful and original room in the whole building is the circular library set in one of the castle's towers. Every element of the Neo-Gothic repertoire was used here: rib vaulting, pointed-arch windows, heavy oak bookcases, wrought-iron door and light fittings and a soaring vaulted ceiling painted and gilded with murals and supported by an ornate central column. The architects achieved a true synthesis between the functional demands of a library and the aesthetic effects of their chosen historical style: the small lead lights of the window filter just the right light for a library, the bookcases which line the walls contain sufficient room for the collection and the octagonal table surrounding the pillar provides ample space on which to lay oversized folios.

The ornament on the furniture, metal mounts and door fittings is composed predominantly of vine motifs. Vines had played an important role in medieval ecclesiastical

iconography, and Neo-Gothic designers regarded this form of decoration as not only highly authentic but also appropriate for secular use.

The Gothic era presented one major problem to the revivalists where domestic interiors were concerned: it possessed no recognizable furniture of the sort that had become indispensable to the citizen of the nineteenth century, from desks down to wastepaper baskets. Despite all efforts, every item of furniture created in the Neo-Gothic style had the same characteristic shortcoming: it remained a modern frame superficially adorned with Gothic-style trimmings such as finials or tracery. There was an additional problem: the thirteenth- and fourteenth-century craftsmen had few of the rich variety of textiles at their disposal that could be produced in the nineteenth century and which contemporary clients had come to regard as essential to their comfort. Thus from the start the Gothic style did not lend itself to purist imitation; Neo-Gothic could never be more than a fanciful interpretation of the real thing. Nevertheless, many champions of the later nineteenth-century Arts and Crafts Movement returned to the Gothic style, responding to the perceived 'honesty' of unpainted wood and the fact that construction was never concealed by ornament.

While some of the problems of authenticity may have been surmountable, this was only at considerable expense and, like the Rococo, Neo-Gothic remained a style for the rich. It was particularly favoured for the castles built in Moravia and Bohemia by the families who had become wealthy through mining. It was also chosen by the older tradition-bound families, many of whom, like the Thurn und Taxis princes in Schloss St Emmeram in Regensburg, or the Hohenzollerns at Schloss Sigmaringen in Swabia, had their ancestral castles refurbished in the Neo-Gothic style in the middle of the century. In Bavaria too, where the theatre designer Domenico Quaglio published his *Die Sammlung der malerischen Burgen der Vorzeit* (*Collection of Picturesque Castles of Times Past*) in 1844–6, the Crown Prince – later King Maximilian II – espoused the Neo-Gothic style, solely in order to distance himself from his authoritarian father, King Ludwig I, who would only countenance the styles of Greek and Roman antiquity.

Left A vaulted corridor lined with suits of armour, as seen in the west wing at the castle of Marienburg, was a recurring feature of German historicist interiors, even in buildings decorated in styles from other periods.
Right The design of the staircase hall at Marienburg accentuates the military aspect of a medieval castle, a reference to the era of the family's great military successes. The monumental Baroque table in the centre came from another Hanoverian palace.

Each of the main rooms at Marienburg contains a massive chimneypiece in varying Gothic-inspired forms. Carved in sandstone from Etz, they were intended to evoke a medieval atmosphere. But the insistence on authenticity had its limits when it came to comfort and in order to ensure a reasonable temperature, a hot-air central-heating system was also installed. (The English-inspired linen-fold oak panelling provided further insulation as well as decorative detail.) And while the wooden ornament on the ceilings and doorways and on the upholstered furniture of the King's Parlour (**opposite, bottom right**) was taken from the repertoire of medieval stone masons, the fabric designs – especially in the Queen's Salon (**opposite bottom left**) – were unmistakably contemporary. The freestanding cast-iron spiral staircase (**opposite top left**) while made from the quintessentially medieval material of iron, is also very much a machine-made technical achievement of the nineteenth century.

Left Franz von Lenbach, one of Munich's most successful society painters, devised this Renaissance-style room – which is named after the Gobelin tapestry that hangs here – entirely for its picturesque effect. The combination of the setting, the gilded archway, the mix of genuine and imitation antiques and the mystical lighting produced just the right atmosphere to express his personality. The reconstruction of 1966 shows the room as it was in 1892, when von Lenbach was enjoying his greatest fame following a visit from the Imperial Chancellor Otto von Bismarck.

Left Textiles played a prominent role in historicist interiors in the nineteenth century and, in the search for authenticity, it was deemed important that contemporary reproductions should imitate examples from the past both in weave and pattern. Thus a special flat-weave design was manufactured for the curtains in the King's Parlour at Marienburg. The design features the stallion, which symbolized Lower Saxony, from the family's coat of arms.

Fully fledged Neo-Gothic style seldom made an appearance in the homes of the bourgeoisie. There it received only glancing recognition with a few additions of tracery to otherwise still Biedermeier-style furniture and perhaps the occasional knick-knack such as an *étagère* or clock case adorned with finials or scrolls fashioned in the latest black wrought-iron work from Berlin.

Problems of authenticity and expense, combined with the re-opening of the debate over whether Gothic was truly the national style for Germany, led, in the late 1860s, to the gradual adoption of the neo-Renaissance style, known at the time as the 'rounded arch style', as Germany's 'new look'. Neo-Renaissance forms were better adapted to the demands of modern construction than were the Gothic variants. Indeed, one of the style's main advantages was that its principles were more suited to the processes of mass production. There were, however, also political reasons why Germans took to this style with such enthusiasm.

When the Franco-Prussian war of 1870–71 ended with the proclamation of Wilhelm I as German Emperor, German patriotism flared up again with renewed vigour. This was helped by the boom in prosperity and production that followed the war. Known as the Gründerzeit (literally, 'The Promoter Years'), the period has since lent its name to a whole category of furniture, sometimes in a pejorative sense. Everyone seemed to want their house decked out in the style of the epoch that the theorists had deemed to be a suitably splendid analogy for the Germany of the latter part of the nineteenth century: the age of Albrecht Dürer, Martin Luther and the noble days of the self-governing cities. The

style belonging to the golden age of the Renaissance was patriotically referred to as Altdeutsch, and enough examples from that period had survived for manufacturers to emulate and supply all the middle-class households of Berlin or Munich with parlours in this 'old German' style. New types of furniture, designed to fit in with prevailing ambience, also appeared on the scene. These included mighty sideboards, high-backed sofas – sometimes built into the wall panelling – and the Berlin 'vertico', a double-doored cupboard topped with a pediment. For all of them, the robust, Renaissance-style ornament was much more fitting than the fragile tracery of the Gothic period.

The high point of the neo-Renaissance period was the exhibition in the Munich Glass Palace of 1876, in which museum pieces from the sixteenth and seventeenth centuries were displayed under the motto 'the works of our fathers' for the inspiration of contemporary designers. There were, however, no hard and fast rules when it came to the decoration of Renaissance-style interiors. Achieving a warm, cosy atmosphere and a picturesque look – both of which were seen as the defining characteristics of the old German period – were more a matter of artistic interpretation. In general, rooms were densely furnished and dimly lit. Bright light was considered undesirable and was softened by heavy, dark-coloured curtains. The predominance of brown tones recommended for the home led Count Harry Kessler – who was later to be one of the people instrumental in setting up the Bauhaus school of design in Weimar – to make fun of the thick lace curtains of the time. He joked that they must be re-stained a brownish hue with coffee after each wash.

Half-height wall panelling was the ideal and doors, never painted white, were made to blend into the scheme through the addition of elaborately carved surrounds. This desire for understated contrasts and subdued lighting may also have been a reaction to what was happening outside on the streets of the new metropolises where rapidly increasing traffic levels were causing a dramatic rise in noise and general disturbance.

The same mood fostered the use of an abundance of textiles, softening the hard edges of windows, tables and chairs and helping to muffle sounds and to filter light. Bright, vulgar colours were frowned upon; instead brown, green and Bordeaux red were the favourites. These helped to convey the patina of age, as in a gallery of old master paintings. Reviving the styles of the past stimulated a new interest in old textiles. Many of these could still be seen in churches and monasteries, and draughtsmen and pattern-gatherers trawled Germany's regions for examples to reproduce. A certain Father Bock achieved notoriety as 'Scissors Bock' because he thought nothing of cutting up the most exquisite old garments into tiny pieces in order to store them efficiently in his archive. The most important factory to produce fabrics in historic patterns was Haas & Söhne of Vienna, from whom it was even possible to order carpets woven after examples from museums.

The importance of interior decoration at that time is indicated by the fact that two highly regarded establishment figures became involved in a public debate about carpet designs. In his influential work of 1871, *Die Kunst im Hause* (*Art in the Home*), the Viennese museum director Jakob von Falke wrote: 'Whoever composes a work for the floor should bear in mind that his drawing will be walked upon, and that he must therefore not lay anything beneath the feet which nature or common decency would not allow us to tread upon.' In *Das deutsche Zimmer der Renaissance* (*The German Room of the Renaissance*) of 1880 the architect Georg Hirth stated categorically that 'even organic patterns are only acceptable if they are completely denaturalized'. Joining the debate, Gottfried Semper expressed his aversion to vivid patterns: 'A carpet will make a bad impression if we are constantly in fear of tripping over the beloved pug dog or stumbling into a shady hole.'

Precisely because they appeared to feature pure ornament alone – and in ignorance of their true meaning – oriental carpets were held in high esteem, and became enormously fashionable after they had first been offered for sale in vast quantities by the Persian participants at the Vienna World Exhibition of 1873.

As the century progressed, historicist styles became mixed with oriental influences and personal preferences, and so became more diffuse and diluted. Lacking any firm direction from establishment figures, the public came to lionize a few self-publicizing society painters who decorated their studios and their houses according to their own eclectic, highly personal tastes. Leading the field as master of his own style was the Munich painter Hans Makart, who settled in Vienna. His atelier – heaped with decorative objects, opulent textiles and both genuine and fake antiques – became a meeting place for the imperial city's high society and, for an entrance fee, could even be visited by ordinary members of the public. A similar phenomenon existed in other capital cities too: in Paris the Hungarian Mihaly Munkacsy and in London Sir Frederick Leighton and Sir Lawrence Alma-Tadema were admired not only as artists but as aesthetes whose tastes in furnishings earned devoted followers.

Above and opposite When he returned to Bavaria in the 1880s after a long stay in Italy, the artist Franz von Lenbach chose to build his house in the centre of Munich in a Tuscan-villa style. Following the Italian tradition, the formal rooms were on the *piano nobile*, or first floor. The decoration of these grand rooms, and those of the artist's studio in the side wing, was devised by von Lenbach with the prime purpose of impressing visitors and potential patrons. Recently restored with the help of archive photographs, they once again have their original appearance of a stage set for a historical play. With their ornate ceilings, the beams of which are carved and gilded, and decorated with Latin inscriptions, the Green Room, the Red Room and Gobelin Room evoke the Italian Renaissance. The Green Room is still arranged as it was by von Lenbach, with his collection of antiques from the fifteenth and sixteenth centuries, closely hung paintings on the walls and oriental carpets on the floor, while the Red Room is hung with his collection of male portraits.

Most of the German artists came from modest backgrounds. Franz von Lenbach, a master of self-invention, started out as a simple Bavarian bricklayer's apprentice but became a highly sought-after society portrait painter. In his villa in Munich, built in the Tuscan style and completed in 1881, he decorated a series of grandiose studios in the Renaissance style. In the central section was a suite of reception rooms in which the chancellor stayed when he was in Munich. Here von Lenbach concocted a symphony of effects, all serving his declared aim of impressing the senses. Ceiling beams carved from dark wood and resting on wide corbels were painted with Latin maxims in gold lettering, evoking the impression of an Italian Renaissance palazzo. The red or green silk papers that clothed the walls provided an atmospheric background for von Lenbach's paintings – his own as well as his valuable collection of Old Masters. He would change his display of art works according to his visitors: one day the emphasis would be on his studies of female nudes interspersed with copies of Rubens's, and on another portraits of distinguished gentlemen or medieval knights would look down from the walls. The Green and the Red Rooms are linked by a grand doorway in the style of a triumphal arch. Made from gilded stucco, it had a copy of an antique relief from a sarcophagus set into it. Another salon was hung with sixteenth-century Burgundian tapestries, the gilded coffered ceiling was decorated with paintings on Renaissance themes, and the cornice was a frieze of the signs of the zodiac. The decoration was a rich combination of Baroque furniture, Eastern objects, oriental carpets, and Gothic and Baroque sculpture.

Visual effect was everything to von Lenbach. It was immaterial to him whether he included original works or merely plaster casts, for example, and he was criticized for instructing his craftsmen to forego expensive materials in favour of cheaper substitutes, such as imitation-mosaic linoleum instead of genuine mosaic floors. Von Lenbach was constantly ordering new accessories for his arrangements from Bernheimer, Munich's leading interiors firm: countless types of ceiling mouldings; vases; picture frames; busts, and, on one occasion, even an entire butterfly collection. In an attempt to imbue the whole ensemble with a suitably theatrical atmosphere and give it the right lighting, he had his own generator installed in the basement in order to supply every room with the latest electric light.

The critics had little influence over the widespread acclaim that von Lenbach's decorative style received. Photographs of his villa were sold as postcards and

published in the *Zeitschrift für Innendekoration* (*Journal for Interior Decoration*) in 1898 as 'an example for everyone's home'. His house featured in contemporary travel guides, which opined that to visit Munich without seeing it would be akin to visiting Rome without an audience with the pope. Von Lenbach himself was vigorous in the defence of his theatrical style of decoration: 'The ultimate purpose of art is after all to quench [rational] thought . . . In fact just as love can inspire such a state in human beings, so too do the beautiful, harmonious surroundings of a noble building.'

As the middle classes became more affluent and aware of the changing fashions in interior decoration, it became possible for firms to sell entire room installations, complete with furniture, carpets, wall coverings and decorative items,

and to show their wares as room settings at the big exhibitions. The sheer range and choice of products becoming available opened the way for the new profession of interior designer or decorator to be established. Often trained as theatre designers, they were able to give advice and combine the work of various individual craftsmen into an overall scheme.

Convention increasingly dictated the style in which a room was decorated. Thus while halls or stairways might contain Renaissance or Gothic elements, smoking rooms were usually furnished with a Turkish flavour; and while 'old German' style was thought suitable for a man's study, neo-Rococo was preferred for a lady's boudoir or the drawing room.

Even when other historicist fashions were on their way out, the light-hearted elegance of the Rococo continued to be regarded as the appropriate style for traditional formal rooms in grander homes. There was understandably some political controversy attached to all the variants of this style: they were seen as the royal French styles of Louis XIV, XV and XVI and at a time when France was still Germany's arch enemy, they were too strong a reminder of France's cultural dominance. The debate about style was also laden with economic considerations. During the second half of the nineteenth century France was the leading exporter of luxury furniture and particularly of

Left Even in the early twentieth century the aristocratic Rococo style of the eighteenth century was still considered the most appropriate one for formal drawing rooms. This explains why a Louis-XVI-style design, by Theodor von Kramer, was chosen by the Faber-Castells, an upwardly mobile manufacturing family, for their newly built palace at Stein, near Nuremberg, in 1906, despite the fact that the other rooms are all very much in the Jugendstil (see pages 146–52).
Right When the last German Emperor, Wilhelm II, was exiled to the Netherlands in 1919, he took quantities of Rococo furnishings with him and made his new drawing room at Haus Doorn close in style to the eighteenth-century apartments he had left behind.

decorative bronzes, all in the traditional royal style. The only way to ensure a market for the products of German craftsmen was to create a demand for them. This was another reason why there was a conscious effort to promote the idea of a national German style and why the applied art societies published pattern books of those Renaissance features that were considered typically German as examples for home furnishings. Techniques from north German and Tyrolean folk art, such as flat or grooved carving, were also espoused so that craftsmen could compete with France's continuing influence. However, the Bavarian king, Ludwig II, remained obsessed by the styles of his beloved absolutist French kings, and he kept whole workshops of skilled craftsmen in Munich busy with commissions in these eighteenth-century

French styles for the decoration of his fairy-tale castles of Linderhof and Herrenchiemsee. As a result, the most complex techniques in porcelain-, tapestry- and furniture-making flourished in Bavaria, but only while Ludwig was alive. This particular variant of historicism came to a swift end with the mysterious death of the royal patron in 1886 since such extravagantly produced carving and textiles could not compete in the ordinary market place in an age of surrogate materials and mass-produced ornament.

Associated with royalty and the nobility, the Rococo continued to be seen as an expression of the finest sensitivities, and so was keenly adopted as a display of aristocratic grandeur by those *nouveaux riches* who made their fortunes during the economic boom of the 1870s. In order to satisfy

increasing demand the factories in the German furniture centres of Berlin and Cologne began to simplify the more complex flourishes, enabling whole items of furniture to be machine-produced in this neo-Rococo style. A contemporary commentator described the fondness for the neo-Rococo, explaining that people loved the idea of luxury furnishings, 'which are much admired in the grand rooms of the aristocracy and yet are within the price range of the middle classes'.

For the aristocracy proper, the French-inspired Rococo style continued to be *de rigueur*. The imperial families of Germany and Austria-Hungary furnished their residences in this style as long as the monarchical self-image remained intact. But by no means were they religiously devoted to the originals. The latest look for the court in Vienna in the late nineteenth century consisted of white-painted neo-Rococo furniture with gilded carving and red velvet upholstery. The Empress Sissi, wife of Franz Joseph I, went as far as having any original Rococo furniture removed from the Vienna Hofburg and replaced with reproductions in the brasher, neo-Rococo style. In Prussia the taste of the imperial family was dictated by its reverence for Frederick the Great. The Emperor lived in the same rooms as his famous forefather, dined off a reproduction of his original china service from KPM Berlin, wrote with the same old-fashioned quills and even deliberately imitated his ancestor's bad spelling. It is not surprising that new apartments in the palaces, such as the suite for the Russian Czar and his wife in the Orangerie, and the Dream Room in Sanssouci, were decorated in neo-Rococo style, as late as 1845 and 1864 respectively.

An example of the late imperial variant of interior style has been preserved in Haus Doorn, in Holland, where the last German emperor, Wilhelm II, spent his exile and died in 1941. When he was forced to leave Germany in 1918, he filled more than fifty train carriages with all the finest examples of furniture and art works that he was allowed to take with him. With their contents he created a court-in-exile in a suite of rooms worthy of a Prussian palace. It contained an extraordinary mix of original and reproduction furniture. For example, the bedroom was furnished with nineteenth-

century Louis-XVI-style furniture inlaid with ceramic medallions from Villeroy & Boch, while the salons contained the most exquisite eighteenth-century originals. Finding the ornament of these antiques a little too understated in comparison to their neo-Rococo companions, Wilhelm thought nothing of having their fragile flower-patterned marquetry enlivened with overpainting. The picturesque effect that he so valued counted for more than the authenticity of the individual objects. After his death it was discovered that images of Christ by revered artists and portraits of the Emperor's relations had been set into countless numbers of the cheapest moulded frames.

Neither in the design of interiors nor in the realm of public architecture could a plausible answer be found to the question of which style was most appropriate for Germany. Even when the debate was joined by kings, such as Maximilian II of Bavaria who set up competitions to decide the matter (unwittingly inviting ridicule when he demanded steep roofs for alpine dwellers, and flat ones for the citizens of the north German lowlands), the result was never entirely convincing. As the century drew to a close the epoch was defined chiefly by its pot-pourri of hybrid styles.

Meanwhile, although the public at large continued to favour an eclectic mixture of historicist styles – even though it seemed increasingly less concerned with genuine historical imitation and more intent on accumulating the greatest possible hoard of all types of ornament – new, more discerning tastes were beginning to emerge. Both architects and an increasingly highly educated body of applied artists were consciously searching for forms that would reflect the new era and the new century ahead.

Left and above In seeking to preserve the atmosphere of his grand Prussian past, Wilhelm II surrounded himself at Haus Doorn in Holland with furniture and mementoes including the late-nineteenth-century bathroom porcelain made by Villeroy & Boch for Potsdam's Neue Palais. Among superb eighteenth-century pieces are reproduction items such as the grandfather clock made *c.* 1900 by the Berlin firm of Julius Zwiener. Even at this late date, the Prussian court was commissioning furniture for its palaces in a Rococo style and this was the style that Wilhelm II sought to emulate.

At the same time that the eclectic, flamboyant interiors of arriviste society painters such as Makart and Lemback became so popular that the decor was accepted almost as a recognized style, some completely different, unreservedly individual German interiors were being made. One of the most idiosyncratic of these was in the house of the carpenter and student of the applied arts, Karl Junker. Such was the eccentricity of its creator that even in his own lifetime he was suspected of insanity. In his house near Lemgo he created an environment that had little to do with the current fashions but which in its own way signified a renunciation of the prevailing conception of a national style. This house, which is both bizarre and impressive, is the homogenous work of an outsider, who is now viewed by architectural historians as a forerunner of Expressionism and by art psychologists as spiritually deranged. Many different legends cling to the history of the extraordinary decoration of the house, including the theory that in its creation Junker was sublimating his sorrow for a failed marriage. What is true is that after he moved into the house in 1891 he led an increasingly isolated life, living and working for his art alone. After his death he left behind not just the house but also almost a thousand paintings, drawings and sculptures.

The basic structure of the house itself follows entirely conventional lines and is in keeping with the regional style of the half-timbered and stone structures inherited from the Renaissance. Even the furniture is based on the historicist furniture types current in the late nineteenth century – the Gothic-effect upholstered armchairs, the sofa mounted with a mirror, or the four-poster bed, for example. However, with an obsession bordering on madness, Junker covered every tiny surface space of these conventional forms – as well as all the structural elements of the house – with paintings and carvings in a style that is reminiscent of Indian or exotic art. But the motifs, both in the details and on the larger surfaces, are mostly Christian. The images are predominantly religious, but there are also many representations of embracing couples. These have been interpreted as an expression of Junker's repressed sexuality – another theory which further fuelled the legend surrounding his allegedly unsuccessful marriage.

The vividly organic, sinewy effect of his designs leads one to imagine a link between Junker's ideas and those of the early Jugendstil artists, whose work – though determinedly anti-historicist – was based on natural forms, although there is no evidence that this lonely artist was in touch with their theories which were just beginning to circulate.

Above If the exterior façade were stripped of all its bizarre surface embellishments, Karl Junker's house would be easily recognized as a conventional half-timbered structure of a type that was common to the Weser region in the nineteenth century and had changed little in its basic form since the seventeenth century.

Opposite The effect of the unrelieved agitation of the surface decoration of the interiors is cumulatively disturbing. Even the upholstery fabric was painted in the same, seemingly crazed, fashion. Designed and made by Junker in the 1890s, the furniture, while conforming to the standard shapes of the time, appears to be constructed of twigs and branches. Although the iron stove (seen top right) would have been from a manufacturer's standard repertory at the time, it is also covered in surface ornament and blends into the overall scheme. Only the range in the kitchen stands out as being purely functional.

Jugendstil, the Werkstätten and the Bauhaus

The quest for a consciously modern style for the new, twentieth century

Designed in 1898 by its owner, the
artist Franz von Stuck, the Music
Room in his villa in Munich is one of
the most impressive music rooms of
the *fin de siècle*, despite the fact that
von Stuck had no personal musical
affiliations (see pages 134–5).

The Jugendstil ideal of the design of a whole building as an integrated concept is reflected in the attention that the artists paid to details. **Left** The door handle designed by Henry van de Velde in *c.* 1902 for the Nietzsche Archive in Weimar appears almost to grow organically out of the wood.
Right The fire screen in the Bayreuth Council Chamber designed by Martin Dülfer in *c.* 1904 is a component of the overall design of the room's structure, furnishings and decoration. The role of the whiplash curves so typical of the early forms of Jugendstil was reduced by Dülfer to ornamental details within a more streamlined, geometric form of Jugendstil.

Towards the end of the 1890s a widespread feeling developed among artistic circles in Europe that the current attitude towards applied arts and interiors was outdated, and that a new approach and a new style were needed for the next century. The imitative styles of historicism that had dominated the nineteenth century should not, it was thought, be allowed to continue; at the same time it was felt that there should be a new respect for the basic qualities of materials and that a conscious effort should be made to improve the quality of life by raising the standards of everyday surroundings.

The questions being asked by German architects and applied artists were the same as those being asked all over Europe. They were the subjects of seemingly endless theoretic, quasi-philosophical pamphlets and debates: What were the forms of the future? How could a home be designed to meet the requirements of modern living? Would it ever be possible to create objects of quality through mass production? Was hand production the sole guarantee of superior goods, or was there no avoiding the use of machinery in the manufacture of furnishings? These questions had preoccupied John Ruskin and William Morris in England as early as the 1860s and had lain at the roots of the English Arts and Crafts Movement of the 1880s; and they continued to occupy the minds of the leading thinkers in the field of applied arts throughout Europe during the first quarter of the new century. In Germany the artists and architects who first grappled with these questions were the protagonists of the Jugendstil ('Youth' style) movement, many of whom were also the founders of the Werkstätten (arts and crafts workshops) and, a little later, of the Werkbund, the first of many societies set up to improve

standards in design and industry, and the Bauhaus school, probably the most important experiment in design education of the twentieth century.

Although Jugendstil – the German variant of the Belgian and French Art Nouveau – is now seen as a quintessentially *fin-de-siècle* decorative style, it was, at the time, part of an aesthetic that set out to revolutionize design for interiors, architecture and household objects. The thinking behind it was a conscious effort to create something entirely new. But more than that, it was an attempt to reconcile the values of the artist with those of industry at a time when new domestic products were being manufactured at a speed that allowed no time to think about form or function. Its ultimate purpose was to unify all elements of life into a perfectly ordered new world of social reform. In outward form it matured from ambitious, floridly organic curvilinear designs to more streamlined, rectilinear designs that pointed the way to the functionalism of the Bauhaus.

The pace and pervasiveness of the new thinking in interiors – and the strength of interest in them – was reflected in the torrent of new magazines that were founded in the 1890s, among them *Innen-Dekoration, Deutsche Kunst und Dekoration, Dekorative Kunst, Kunst und Handwerk* and *Jugend,* which gave its name to the style.

Munich was the birthplace of many of these new endeavours. During the last two decades of the nineteenth century it became the 'design centre' of Germany, a sort of cultural cousin to the imperial and political capital of Berlin. Here, in 1898, a group of Jugendstil artists, including Hermann Obrist, Martin Dülfer and Richard Riemerschmid, founded

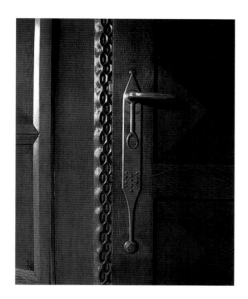

Left and right Built at the beginning of the twentieth century by consciously up-to-date clients, the Schloss Faber-Castell is a showcase of contemporary design. There are examples of the more pronounced floral imagery of Jugendstil, inspired by the French Art Nouveau, on some of its ceilings (see page 150) and on details such as this chamois-leather-covered jewellery box, from a Nuremburg metalwork factory, with its patinized alloy mounts . However, it also includes the work of the designer Bruno Paul, whose own brand of Jugendstil broke new ground with the type of restrained ornament seen on the study door handle from c. 1905 mounted on a relief-edged oak door.

the Vereinigte Werkstätten (United Workshops for Art and Craft) in response to the flood of poor-quality products that were feeding a new consumer market. Modelled on the nineteenth-century English guilds such as Charles Ashbee's or the workshops founded by William Morris, this association of artists, craftsmen and private patrons saw itself as an answer to the quest for well-designed, integrated interiors, providing high-quality hand-crafted furnishings and ornament. Special fields such as ceramics or textiles (termed the 'minor arts') were released from their isolation and combined with the 'free' arts in an attempt to create interiors appropriate for the modern world. Following the Munich examples, the Deutsche Werkstätten in Dresden were founded later that year.

The products of these workshops were intended chiefly for the ordinary middle classes, and the first advertising leaflet set great store by the fact that the goods were 'manufactured on German soil by the hand of German artists', and were 'the expression of German emotions and sensibility'. But what appeared to be a thoroughly nationalistic sentiment was soon refuted by a very different reality. Based on a system whereby each designer would profit from an economic share in the end product, the organization soon attracted a wide spectrum of internationally renowned creative talents, including Vienna-born Josef Maria Olbrich, Josef Hoffman, the founder of the Wiener Werkstätte, Charles Rennie Mackintosh from Scotland and the English architect Baillie Scott. In fact, united by their declared aim of delivering quality in all aspects of domestic design, from the architectural shell to the smallest decorative detail, all the European practitioners of the emerging style worked in close contact with each other.

The early Jugendstil designs may have been pioneering in their modernity, and certainly won copious awards at exhibitions, but many required such a high degree of skilled craftsmanship to manufacture that they could be produced only with the aid of wealthy patrons. And some of the designs, like those by Bernhard Pankok, with lush ornament based on flower and plant forms, were not suitable for mass production nor could be they be made sturdily enough by hand to be of practical use. Indeed, some of the early designers, including the philosopher August Endell and the doctor Hermann Obrist, came from other disciplines and had no understanding of their materials or of joinery. It was to be several years before artists designed furniture or household goods that were suitable for industrial production.

One of the most prominent patrons of early Jugenstil was Grand Duke Ernst Ludwig von Hessen-Darmstadt. He had the means to commission furniture by Baillie Scott and Ashbee and he employed leading designers such as Olbrich and Peter Behrens to work at the artists' colony that he founded on a hillside at Darmstadt in 1899. There they created houses for themselves that were a perfect synthesis of modern architecture and luxurious yet aesthetic interiors, but although their furniture and ornament, designed in a new, more geometric form of Jugenstil, had attracted international attention by 1901, most were still exquisite, one-off designs; few could afford them and they were quite unsuitable as prototypes for industry. This failure to provide any commercially viable work led Behrens to seek stimulation elsewhere, and he left Darmstadt in 1902 though the colony did not close down until 1914.

While the Jugendstil artists in Munich were pursuing their avant-garde ideas, the cultural life of Munich's high society continued to be defined chiefly by the influence of a few successful mainstream artists including Franz von Lenbach and Franz von Stuck. Known in their own day as 'painter princes', they were revered as arbiters of taste, and their houses were considered the epitome of artistic refinement. Planned like a stage set down to the last detail, they were as much a departure from conventional interior design as were the works of the Jugendstil movement, but because they were so highly personal, they were to have little continuing influence.

In contrast to von Lenbach, Franz von Stuck turned his back on the fashion for historicism and sought to express his personality in completely new forms. Von Stuck, one of Munich's favourite portraitists at the turn of the century, started life as the son of a miller but during the course of a spectacular career he became a multimillionaire and acquired an aristocratic title, and his villa became a focus for high society not just in Munich but throughout Germany. It was greatly admired in its time as the product of an individual's creative powers – von Stuck himself designed the heavy, square exterior as well as the elegant interior, and painted all the detailed wall decorations inside. Thus the villa belongs in the tradition of self-designed artists' houses which had begun in 1859 with William Morris's Red House, and was continued in Bloemenwerf, Henry van de Velde's Brussels house of 1896, and the houses designed by the artists Olbrich and Behrens for themselves at Darmstadt in 1901. The reformers and von Stuck shared one goal: to design a fully integrated environment. However, von Stuck's house was different in an important way: while those of the others were material expressions of the occupants' crusading principles, attempts to realize their visions of a life in harmony with art and to change the attitudes of their fellow humans through a new approach to interior design, von Stuck's had no greater purpose than to express his own exuberant personality.

Shrouded in a permanent gloom, the interior was decorated with a combination of reliefs and statues based on Classical themes (chosen for their specific associations rather than any aesthetic value) and von Stuck's own erotic paintings, and filled with artistic 'altars' that gave it a mystical atmosphere. However, the structure of each room is characterized by the same principles of symmetry that were to be central to the geometric designs of the later Jugendstil period, and the excess of decorative objects – the drapery, antiques or historicist furniture – found in many of his contemporaries' homes is absent. Instead, the fragile, sparingly placed furniture that he designed himself is faintly reminiscent of Classical forms and has elements that are a foretaste of late Jugendstil designs. His furniture was shown and received a gold medal at the Paris Exhibition of 1900. Yet von Stuck was disdainful of the more functional furniture being produced at the same time by artists involved with the Vereinigte Werkstätten, commenting that he found most of it 'simply ugly'. The house was later to attract much criticism, both as a monument to a decadent *fin-de-siècle* spirit and for a layout that revealed complete ignorance of any normal domestic requirements (von Stuck's descendants were made uncomfortably aware of its hopelessly impractical aspects); there were no imitators of his style.

Above Glimpsed from the colonnaded portico of the Villa Stuck in Munich is the lifesize bronze statue of a female *Riding Amazon* by Franz von Stuck. Though cast in 1913, it was placed at the villa's entrance only in 1936.
Opposite There is a pagan air as well as a decadent theatricality about the sumptuous decorations of the public rooms of the Villa Stuck, which is accentuated by the sombre lighting, and the use of deep, intense colours set off by gold highlights.
Top left The Orpheus niche (taking its name from the quote 'When Orpheus sang, the animals of the earth, the birds in the sky and the fish in the sea came to listen') in the Music Room contains a cast of a sculpture of Artemis from Pompeii, which was painted by von Stuck. The strictly geometric divisions on the walls are echoed in the costly exotic wood floor.
Top right The walls of the drawing room glow gold with Venetian mosaics.
Bottom left The cast of Athena was also painted for increased dramatic effect.
Bottom right The 1897 model for the *Riding Amazon* stands in front of von Stuck's painting of *The Guardian of Paradise*, a work much celebrated in Munich at the turn of the century.

Left The Nietzsche Archive is housed in a suite of rooms on the ground floor of the Villa Silberblick in Weimar, where Nietzsche lived with his sister, Elisabeth Förster-Nietzsche, from 1897 until he died in 1900.
Right Typical of Van de Velde's own interpretation of Jugendstil is the combination of organic and geometric forms, here seen in the brass and copper fittings on the snow-dusted vestibule doors.
Opposite Even in the entrance hall, the clarity of Henry van de Velde's overall design for the Archive is apparent. He always paid particular attention to the design of such details as the metal coat hooks and door handles.

In Weimar, which was once a prominent literary city but in the nineteenth century had sunk into virtual insignificance, the beginning of a cultural renaissance was signalled by the design of the Nietzsche Archive 1903 by the architect and designer Henry van de Velde. Van de Velde had made his name in his native Belgium in the 1890s. He had spent some time in Paris, where the art dealer Samuel (originally Siegfried – he was German-born) Bing sought unsuccessfully to promote his talents in his gallery La Maison de L'Art Nouveau, which also showed the work of Guimard, Gallé and Tiffany, and then moved to Berlin in 1900. In 1902 Count Kessler, one of the most influential patrons of the Jugendstil, invited van de Velde to Weimar as principal of the Grand Duchy of Saxony's new School of Applied Arts. In doing so he hoped that this little regional capital might follow the Darmstadt model and become a centre of progressive German art. Certainly van de Velde brought a breath of fresh air into the little town stultified by conservative historicism. He began by setting up craft workshops, assisting them financially with the proceeds from his many private commissions; and by placing his furniture orders with local artisans, such as the Scheidemantel firm, he helped them to achieve an undreamt-of prosperity. Van de Velde went on to become one of the founders of the Deutsche Werkbund; it was also van de Velde who, in 1915, suggested that Walter Gropius should establish a 'school providing artistic guidance for industry, trade and craft'. This institution eventually materialized as the Bauhaus, which was to be responsible for one of the most important chapters in the international history of design in the twentieth century.

But van de Velde was himself somewhat hazy – indeed almost contrary – in his artistic allegiances. He had disparagingly used the term 'Palais' to describe von Stuck's villa in Munich, and in Brussels he had shown himself to be influenced by Russian anarchists, declaring, 'Anything that benefits only an individual is virtually useless, and a future society will only value the things that are of some use.' And yet he was to go on to be employed almost exclusively by wealthy Germans, producing superb interiors and important designs of outstanding originality that were far from being suitable for the rational processes of commercial mass production.

Van de Velde chose his materials to pander to the tastes of his clients. As a result he produced very little furniture in pine: at the very least it had to be beech, but better still oak or expensive tropical woods such as mahogany, sandalwood or jacaranda. Metal mounts and fittings, which played an important role in his interiors, were made of equally costly materials, including silver – or even gold – plate, the latter having the advantage over brass of not tarnishing. The élitist quality to his interiors was expressed perfectly by a contemporary assessing the study that van de Velde had designed for Count Kessler: 'This has been made for a man who never makes an error of judgement!'

Given this attitude, it is hardly surprising that van de Velde played little part in the contemporary debates over the socio-political purpose of modern design. In later years he deliberately distanced himself from the examples of John Ruskin and William Morris, whom he had at first admired, but who in his view had wasted their time, both on long-winded aesthetic and social theses and on an unproductive dilettantism. He contradicted the notion, held dear by most of the Jugendstil artists, that materials themselves had a natural beauty which it was the duty of the designer to emphasize without undue embellishment: 'No material is inherently beautiful ... wood, metal, stone and precious stones owe their distinctive beauty to the life bestowed upon them by the particular process, the marks of the tools and the various ways in which the enthusiastic passion or the sensibilities of whoever is working on them are expressed.'

Despite repeated refusals to create what he regarded as inferior designs in order that they could be mass-produced,

van de Velde held firm to the idea of 'Gesamtkunstwerk', that is the notion of the total environment as a complete work of art, such as he had achieved in his own house on the outskirts of Brussels. For each of his patrons he designed everything from the architectural shell of the building to the coat hooks inside it, including the crockery and any number of other items used for everyday life in the house, such as flower vases, letter-openers, the pattern on a car blanket or even a pipe.

Apart from his own house in Weimar, Hohe Pappeln, van de Velde's most significant projects during his time in Weimar were the Villa Esche for a Chemnitz manufacturer and the redesign of the villa that had belonged to one of Germany's great intellectuals, the Villa Silberblick. It was here that the philosopher Friedrich Nietzsche had spent the last three years if his life, when his mind was unbalanced, before his death in 1900. His ambitious sister Elisabeth Förster-Nietzsche, whose purpose in life seems to have been the cultivation and idolization – to the point of falsification – of her adored brother's oeuvre, decided in 1902 to have the ground floor of the house remodelled as a shrine to his memory. While he was alive she had held spine-chilling séances there, during which she had presented her astonished guests with the sight of her mentally incapacitated brother dressed in a Roman toga

Left Designed by van de Velde in 1903, the Nietzsche Archive has recently been restored to its original, pristine condition. Even the grey-blue carpet and the strawberry-crush coloured upholstery have been rewoven. The modernity of the furniture, manufactured by the Scheidemantel firm of court joiners in Weimar, has come into its own once again. The simple, sweeping lines of the upholstered banquette and the chairs are echoed by the coving of the ceiling. Van de Velde also designed the piano and the three-sided work table with the raised brass fruit bowl.

and silhouetted behind violet curtains. With even less self-awareness she characterized herself as the high priestess and guardian of Nietzsche's work.

Elisabeth entrusted the design of the rooms that would become the permanent Nietzsche Archive to van de Velde. His designs were executed to his usual high standards, with the result that the cost of decorating just one ground-floor room came to considerably more than the villa's original purchase price. On this matter however the architect felt himself to be at one with the dead philosopher: 'Did Nietzsche not instigate the scheme himself?' he asked. 'The essence of culture is perfection, the utmost sophistication and refinement in all things.'

The tone of this particular room is defined by a balance of subtle luxury and functional clarity. The beech frames of the furniture match the fitted bookshelves and unpainted frames of the windows and doors. One of the most distinctive features is the way in which the vertical struts that enclose the window surrounds and divide the bookcases continue upwards so that they become an integral part of the fluted coving of the ceiling. This was one of van de Velde's most original, and favourite, devices in his quest for a more unified overall design. He planned something similar for the director's room in Weimar's Grand-Ducal Museum, a commission which never went ahead.

In Elisabeth Förster-Nietzsche's time the main archive room was crammed with all manner of relics and mementoes of her brother's life and work, including his death mask, and although it has been restored so that van de Velde's designs are now the chief focus, Max Klinger's bust of the philosopher, placed on a high marble pedestal against the light, still gives the effect of a memorial room. Until her death in 1935 Elisabeth used this room to receive the great intellectuals of the Weimar Republic, as well as those who were later to abuse her brother's name and use his reputation for their own political purposes; she was even flattered to receive a visit from Adolf Hitler.

Right Resplendent above the wall stove with its elaborate brass doors is the prominent initial 'N' for Nietzsche, likewise in brass and a sign of the almost maniacal reverence displayed by his sister in commissioning these rooms.

Meanwhile van de Velde's contemporaries in Munich were finding international recognition for their work. At the 1904 World Exhibition in St Louis, USA, Martin Dülfer, Bruno Paul and the Rank brothers, three Munich architectural practices, showed schemes for three interiors for the government building in Bayreuth. The rooms – an office and a Reception Room for the President, and the State Council Chamber – each won a prize at the exhibition: the reception room designed by the Rank brothers received the silver medal; and Paul's office and Dülfer's council chamber were jointly awarded the Grand Prix. Placed *in situ* and still in use today, the interiors are still virtually in their original state, and are some of the very few surviving examples of complete room designs from the late Jugendstil period. The defining feature of all three is the clarity of their functional lines: these were a new departure, a strong contrast to the sinuously curving confections, typical of French Art Nouveau, that were still so popular at that time. There is just a hint of the earlier style on some of the door handles, but the ceilings are quite plain: the organically inspired ceiling mouldings that had been fashionable until then were completely dispensed with.

The other dominant components are the abundant use of wood in a variety of colours, and the use of geometric decoration in the form of inlaid rhomboids and squares within the wood. In the Council Chamber the decoratively stitched backs of the leather sofas and the mantels of beaten bronze protecting the grey marble pillars bring an almost Gothic touch to the room. When they were brand-new, the effect of the colours in all of these rooms would have been even more striking than it is today. The oak panelling in the President's Office, and the maple panelling in the Reception Room, which has now turned various shades of brown, was once stained a delicate pale grey. This would have made a better contrast to the deep blue covers of the seating in the Reception Room. And, to the satisfaction of the judges at the St Louis Exhibition, this room was originally finished off by a dazzlingly rich yellow carpet.

The President's Office was originally entirely furnished in grey-stained oak and was fitted with a carpet patterned with wildflowers. In this room, Bruno Paul used an elegant device which he was also to employ on several other occasions. Leather sofas were combined with a corner cabinet, and the whole neatly framed by the wooden panelling on the walls. Complemented by a small reading table or comfortable armchairs (as it was when it was first installed at Bayreuth), the result was a niche of informal privacy and comfort. Paul also designed fitted bookshelves for this room, and was later to have the opportunity to perfect his technique for constructing built-in furniture when he was commissioned by the north German shipping company Lloyd's to furnish their luxury steamers with suitably grand suites in 1908. His designs for this room in Bayreuth were to inspire a new and progressive attitude to the use of space, not only in his own work but also in that of his contemporaries.

The President's Office designed by Bruno Paul (**left**) and the Reception Room designed by Franz and Josef Rank (**right**) for the Bayreuth government building met with great acclaim for their innovative, uncluttered lines when they were exhibited at the 1904 World Exhibition in St Louis. In the office the corner seating arrangement, with a built-in corner cupboard and low table, was a device which Paul was to employ again and again. All the components of the room were built by the Munich Werkstätten. The inlaid wainscotting and the *en suite* furniture in the Reception Room were executed by the Ballin factory of court joiners in Munich. The floor was originally covered with a bright yellow carpet.

Right and left The restrained functionality of late Jugendstil, with its geometric motifs, can be seen to particular effect in the Bayreuth Council Chamber designed by the architect Martin Dülfer. All the elements of this room, from the ceiling to the fireguards, were his designs. His use of pierced beaten bronze as a decorative cladding around the pillars was highly original. The patterns on these are echoed in the pillars at the sides of the leather-upholstered high-backed settle. All the wooden furniture in this room was executed by the Bayreuth firm of court joiners, J. A. Eysser, which was internationally known for the high quality of its work. The coats of arms displayed as inlay in the wainscot panelling of mahogany belong to the Upper Franconian cities which were represented at the council; the marble relief above the fireplace is a portrait of the Prince Regent, Luitpold of Bavaria .

The Bayreuth office was so admired that, not long after it was exhibited, the same room was commissioned by the Faber-Castell family for their castle, in Stein, near Nuremberg. This wealthy family – whose pencils, produced in the factory adjacent to the castle, are still sold throughout the world today – was a typical example of the patrons who employed avant-garde artists in the design of their homes. Feeling the need to prove their social status they were inclined towards an ostentatious sort of eclecticism – as is well illustrated by the castle's various period-style rooms – but they also had

the sophistication to be open to new ideas and the means to commission the best designers. In Bruno Paul they found someone who had something new to offer: his designs were innovative, elegant and purist in form (and his work for the Schloss Faber-Castell was to make him one of the most sought-after designers during the 1910s and 20s).

The Faber family had risen during the nineteenth century from craftsmen roots to the ranks of the Bavarian industrial aristocracy. Because there were no male heirs, Baroness Ottilie inherited her grandfather's estate and when she

Left The nursery at Schloss Faber-Castell was designed by Bruno Paul specifically for children's use. Executed by the Eysser firm in Bayreuth, the furniture is small in proportion, and has no sharp corners. It was painted white so that it would reflect all the available light and also look clean and bright – a new idea that was a direct contrast to the dark rooms and furnishings of the historicist era. The floor is covered with a flower-patterned linoleum, which would have been warmer, softer and easier to keep clean than wood. The frieze on the walls depicts the changing seasons. The toys now on display are just some of those that remain from the heaps that came for the children from the famous Nuremberg toy factories of the Fleischmann Brothers, the Bing Brothers and C. Hacker.
Right Designed by the castle's architect, Theodor von Kramer, so that light comes in from two sides, the stairwell contains a wealth of impressive details: each of the marble-faced pillars has a different capital, and there are reflective gold mosaics on the wall above the arches. The marble figure in the hall is a copy of a Classical statue of Venus.

married a count from the old Castell line of Franconian noblemen which had fallen on hard times, they built a castle of impressive proportions with the deliberate intention of celebrating their new family line and advertising their newly eminent position in society. The old-fashioned, rigidly conservative precepts that the Count brought to the marriage are evident in the way in which the castle's rooms are organized. There was no single room for the use of all the family; there were separate libraries, as well as separate bathrooms, for husband and wife; and the children played in their own nursery in the care of governesses. The Count and Countess lived increasingly separate lives until Ottilie sought solace in the arms of another aristocrat, the sad story ending in her being humiliatingly banished from the castle, which had been financed by her family's fortunes. Thereafter the castle was scarcely used and today it numbers among Germany's most important collections of historic interiors.

Thanks to the financial success of the firm, the Faber-Castells were able to spend what was, for the early 1900s, the astronomical sum of three million gold marks to decorate and furnish the castle. They were also able to employ the best designers, including Bruno Paul. His most beautiful, most original room – every detail exudes understatement, grace and elegance – is Ottilie's 'Lemon Room' – mistakenly named, as both the furniture and panelling are in fact made from luxurious rosewood veneers (although they were once thought to be from lemon-tree wood). The purpose of this room was laid down in writing: it was for 'the woman of the house to spend time in, when free from the demands of children, domestic chores or social duties, to devote herself to intellectual pursuits, to read, to play music or simply to busy herself with fine handiwork'.

Keeping this brief in mind, Bruno Paul drew on the 'cabin style' that he had developed in his work on ocean liners. He gave the comparatively large room a degree of intimacy by dividing it into separate, cosy niches, and concealed the corners of the room behind diagonally set wall mirrors that reflected the light. The delicate furnishings, which have survived virtually intact, have a very feminine look: the turquoise-blue upholstery fabric was once echoed by the fabric wall covering in the same colour and by the green, blue and white glass of the skylights.

The bathrooms in the castle were designed by its architect, Theodor von Kramer, and are outstanding examples of the Jugendstil approach to form and function. In terms of function they offered the highest degree of hygiene and comfort, and in terms of form they were conceived as integral works of art, down to the smallest details such as plug holes or soap dishes. They also revealed a progressive functionalism that was characteristic of Jugendstil interiors after the style's initial experimental stage: an unusual ornamental effect was achieved by the shape and position of the exposed water pipes, which served as heated towel rails, in front of silver-painted stucco and marble decoration. In keeping with the room's functions, the marble reliefs and mosaic roundels portray aquatic themes, including mythological scenes with Poseidon and dolphins.

The Count's bathroom is characterized by its colour scheme of silver with touches of turquoise while in the Countess's bathroom gold dominates. Both have immense, walk-in marble sunken baths. There is a hugely elaborate shower contraption in the Count's bathroom, but no such equivalent in Ottilie's: at the turn of the century a bath was the only means of ablution considered appropriate for ladies. All the same, as well as the usual hot and cold taps, the Countess was also provided with the innovative addition of a hand-held shower attachment for hair washing. The balance of streamlined function and restrained ornament that so fascinates us today was, at the time, heavily cluttered: contemporary photographs show that the bathrooms were made to look more 'lived in' by the addition of curtains, rugs, upholstered chairs and pot plants.

Opposite above The slimline marble and brass-clad stove in the so-called Lemon Room at Schloss Faber-Castell was designed by Bruno Paul. The unmistakably *fin-de-siècle* bust portrays Poetry.
Opposite below On either side of the door into the Lemon Room is the fitted furniture that became the hallmark of Paul's interior design.
Below The Music Room at Schloss Faber-Castell is lined with maple panels and inlaid with mother of pearl, metal and mahogany. The panelling was kept at half height so as not to spoil the acoustics.

Previous pages The silvery-grey bathroom for the Count and the golden-yellow one for the Countess were manufactured to designs by Theodor von Kramer. Masterpieces of Jugendstil interior design, they are also examples of the latest sanitary equipment, which was manufactured by Villeroy & Boch and MAN, both of which are still internationally known.

These pages The opulent detailing in Ottilie's bathroom includes marble-cladding and exquisitely cut marble decoration, a relief of Venus at her bath, bevelled mirror glass, crystal-drop chandeliers and vigorous Jugendstil designs in stucco on the ceiling.

Bruno Paul was one of the designers who had worked with the Vereinigte Werkstätten from their inception in 1898, and he was to work closely with these workshops throughout his career. In 1908, for example, they took on the fabrication of the ship fittings that he designed for Lloyd's (from which so-called 'steamer' or 'cabin-style' furniture originates).

When they were first set up, the Werkstätten were employed chiefly in supplying artist-designed domestic furnishings for wealthy clients, but they soon expanded, developing into big businesses with several hundred collaborative workers between them. The intensive creative and financial investment and extensive output involved in these demanded a rational structure that was far removed from the original conception of the Werkstätten as a series of small cooperatives.

Related to these developments were the constant debates between artists and craftsmen, which intensified after the end of the First World War, over how to produce 'The Low-cost Home' (as one of the treatises to be published on the subject was entitled). Seminal in this debate was Hermann Muthesius. He had been sent to London as Germany's architectural attaché in 1896, where he soon observed the way that the guilds of craftsmen were organized there, and also recognized the potential of machine production. As a result, on his return to Germany he was instrumental in setting up the German Werkbund in 1907. Like the Werkstätten, this was also loosely modelled on the English guild system, but was intended not just to unite artists and craftsmen with patrons, but to unite arts and crafts with industry, and also to promote the standardization of interior design to make it suitable for machine manufacture. With great perspicacity Muthesius recommended Bruno Paul as director of the School of Art and Craft in Berlin and Peter Behrens as head of the one in Düsseldorf. Both men actively pursued the ideas inherent in the Werkbund principles; Behrens, who was particularly interested in the commercial value of good design, was made consultant and later chief designer for the electrical giant, AEG.

Left Painted furniture in strong, single colours was integral to the Jugendstil vision of simplicity and clarity. The choice of colour, however, was often rooted in traditional wisdom, such as the belief that blue warded off flies and was therefore particularly appropriate in kitchens – as for example on this dresser in the Villa Brey, designed by Emanuel von Seidl (**top**), or in purely practical notions, such as white being known to add brightness to a room, as in this white-lacquered furniture in a bedroom designed by the architect Richard Riemerschmid for Dr Carl's country house (**bottom**).

The standardized furniture designed by Paul, among others, and the new materials such as plywood, which was used in the Deutsche Werkstätten in Dresden, made it possible to produce items of high quality at a reasonable cost. New fabrics too, were created to meet modern needs. Designed in the textile studios attached to each production workshop, they could be adapted for various uses, whether for curtains or for upholstery. Usually printed in small-scale abstract or geometric patterns and in only one or two colours, they had a simple overall effect that served to underline the clarity of a room or the function of an item of furniture.

During his posting in London, Muthesius had also become interested in the new architectural theories being promoted there, and had produced various essays on the English art of building. The most influential of these was 'The Modern Country House and its Internal Design' of 1904–5 which extolled the virtues of the new ideals of domestic architecture. It offered inspiration to the reforms that were beginning to take place in Germany in response to a way of life which, according to forward-thinkers and Jugendstil protagonists, was being reduced by increasing urbanization and industrialization to little more than a succession of mechanical rituals. One of the outcomes of the reform movement was the building of garden cities – housing surrounded by gardens and parks on the outskirts of large towns, where industry was limited but from where places of work could easily be reached; and one of the principal achievements of the Deutsche Werkstätten was the construction of the garden city of Dresden-Hellerau, begun in 1907.

At about the same time, a new attitude arose among the upper middle classes in Germany towards life on the land, which encompassed a romantic attachment to native soil and a recognition of the simple beauty of rural dwellings. The consequent demands for housing that met these ideals presented a fresh set of architectural challenges, and Muthesius's reports from England also inspired the creation of houses that were the architectural antidote to the tradition of historicist villas.

Right The spirit of a return to rural roots that is evident in the distinctive 'Bavarian folk' flavour characterizing the interiors of many country houses and holiday homes in southern Germany at the beginning of the twentieth century is seen in the solid staircase designed by Emanuel von Seidl in 1903–5 for the Villa Brey (**top**). The 'Deutsche Werkstätten' inscription on the plaque at the entrance to the architect Niemeyer's country house (**bottom**) refers to the collaborative craft workshops which made, to his designs, many of the furnishings for this house between 1913 and 1921.

The villa designed by Richard Riemerschmid for the industrial chemist and publisher Dr Carl is an authentic example of the new style of middle-class country house. Occupied today by Dr Carl's descendants, it was built in 1910 in Feldafing, near Munich, close to a prominent community of aristocrats, heads of industry, professors, art dealers and property developers who had established a colony there in 1897 on the shores of a particularly beautiful stretch of Lake Starnberg. Dr Carl already owned several pieces of furniture by Riemerschmid and was well acquainted with his clear, purist style.

Riemerschmid was a highly accomplished architect who also produced designs for furniture, glass and ceramics that were all distinguished by both their originality and an unerring practicality. He was another of the artists involved in setting up the Vereinigte Werkstätten in Munich. During the course of his career his work progressed from being influenced by early Jugendstil ideas to being governed by the principles of the German Werkbund. His first big success was the much-fêted 'Room of an Art-lover' for the Paris Exhibition of 1900, which was dominated by the sinuous lines of early Jugendstil; but then Riemerschmid began to develop a more austere, reductive style, with a preference for revealed construction and working methods which emphasized the natural qualities of his materials. For example, his fondness for pine, untreated except for a heavy brushing to raise the grain, led one of his contemporaries to remark that one might almost think that 'the German forest had moved into interior design'. In combining the use of local materials with both a logistical approach to the construction of his furniture and elements of folk art, Riemerschmid took Jugendstil into a new dimension. In 1909 the leading English design periodical *The Studio* described him, rightly, as 'one of the leaders of modern German applied art'. Through his collaboration with various Werkstätten and later under the auspices of the German Werkbund, Riemerschmid turned his attention to the new discipline of designing standard furniture for commercial manufacture, becoming one of the first Germans, with Behrens and Paul, to be aware of the parameters of machine production.

Riemerschmid also saw himself as a creator of integrated interiors, of which sadly only a very few have survived. The most significant is the one for Dr Carl in Feldafing. In the search for an aesthetic unity, Dr Carl commissioned Riemerschmid to design not only the external structure, including the garden, but – with the exception of the dining room which was based on designs by Bruno Paul – all the internal space as well. This brief extended beyond the usual doors and windows, bathrooms and kitchen, to include overall responsibility for the furniture and all details, including radiator covers, handles, locks and hinges for furniture, loose furnishings, curtains and even the crockery.

The bedroom on the first floor is particularly attractive. Flooded with light, painted white and with its original green fitted carpet, it has a bright, cheerful air that works especially well in the rural setting that is visible through windows on two sides of the room. The console that runs along beneath the windows (a feature which Riemerschmid, who had also designed for a shipping company, had used in the cabins of an express steamer) makes a well-lit dressing table. One of Riemerschmid's overriding concerns in the design of this house was that all the main rooms should be arranged so that they let in as much light as possible at all times of the day, a concern which was acknowledged by the contemporary design press: 'There should be no house content simply cosying up to rural forms; but the spacious residence of an urban gentleman whose pampered living conditions have been recreated here in the country. And I mean in the country: light, air, space; a luxurious invitation to stretch out one's entire being, both inwardly and outwardly.' Simple wooden floors are combined with glazed wall tiles in strong colours, and innovative radiator 'curtains', fashioned of little discs of brass tied together with wire and beads, move constantly in the warm air, winking in the light. All this contributed to a style which was neither clumsily 'folksy' nor reminiscent of any previous style. Exhibited in Paris, at the Salon d'Automne of 1910, before being installed, these interiors won great acclaim as a unrivalled example of the new German style, despite the proviso that it would be 'impossible to envisage a Parisian woman in these rooms'.

Opposite The now very over-grown door of the country house that Richard Riemerschmid designed for Dr Carl on the shore of Lake Starnberg in 1910.
Right Like the other rooms, the light-filled bedroom has been preserved in its original state. The white-painted fitted pine cupboards are similar in design to Bruno Paul's cabin fittings for luxury steamers.

Overleaf The emphatic clarity in the construction of the furniture in the living room is typical of Riemerschmid. The rectilinear design of the chairs blends well with the geometrically laid walnut veneers of the sideboards. The original rice-straw matting on the walls and the simple wooden floorboards are characteristic of Riemerschmid's own particular brand of country-house style. Standing on the sideboard are glasses designed by Riemerschmid, and also his famous Mettlach punch bowl of 1902. This bowl displayed the use of abstract design in applied art years before the artist Wassily Kandinsky painted his first abstract works.

One of the most successful villa architects in south Germany at the turn of the century was Emanuel von Seidl. The favourite architect of Munich's upper classes, leader of the German delegation at various international trade exhibitions, he was, with his brother Gabriel, one of the most important protagonists of a more romantic country house style that had a distinctively Bavarian flavour. Like Riemerschmid, he liked to plan the interiors of the houses that he designed down to the smallest detail – his clients could order even household utensils and bed linen directly from him. Some of these items he designed himself; others he bought in from various other sources, acting as coordinating interior designer.

In 1903–05 Emanuel von Seidl undertook a commission to extend what had been a hunting lodge into a substantial country house for Captain Ludwig Brey (once proprietor of the world-famous Löwenbrau breweries; the house was later bought by a director of another brewery, whose family still own it). The numerous sets of antlers both outside and in are a reminder of the building's original function. In common with most of the von Seidls' commissions, the Villa Brey is set in stunningly beautiful surroundings. It stands in an extensive stretch of parkland between Lake Staffel and Murnau Moor, and has an awe-inspiring view over the Alps in the distance. The rooms are furnished in an atmospheric variant of late Jugendstil and make constant reference to their Bavarian surroundings. The style of the house, highly popular at the time, is characterized by a vernacular cosiness and a noble restraint more in the spirit of English interiors, dispensing with any need for impressive status symbols.

Above and right Set before a breathtaking backdrop of Alpine scenery, the Villa Brey, a former hunting lodge, remodelled in 1903–5 to plans of Emanuel von Seidl, represents a picturesquely historicist variant of Jugendstil. The same spirit is present in the landscaped garden and terrace. The garden furniture, designed by von Seidl, was later produced in quantity by the well-known firm of Rheinau.

Right The sets of antlers in the so-called Hunting Room are a reminder of the villa's original function, while the old beer mugs are souvenirs of the owner's breweries. Everything in this room was either designed or chosen personally by von Seidl.

This page The kitchen of Villa Brey, preserved in its original 1905 state, gives us an inkling of the laborious nature of domestic work of those days, even in a wealthy, sophisticated household.
Opposite All the bedroom furniture was designed by Emanuel von Seidl; the white-painted bedside table was one of his most successful Jugendstil designs and appeared in several of the villas that he designed, including his own country house. Von Seidl attached great importance to the blending of colour and ornament. The rose frieze (which is repeated in a glazed stove elsewhere in the room) picks up the colours of both the wallpaper and the curtains. Over the bed hangs a portrait painted by Munich artist Bauriedl in 1913, of Marianne, mother of the current owner.

Left, right and below The architect Niemeyer designed his summer house as well as most of the individual furnishings inside, which he had made up by the Deutsche Werkstätten. Not only the furniture, but also the carpet, the table linen and the almost Expressionist tiled stove executed by Franz Reither in 1921 were all based on his designs. The stove, which has echoes of early seventeenth-century Bavarian stoves, includes illustrations of saints and allegorical scenes to do with water – a direct allusion to the nearby lake and the wet climate.

Not far away from the Villa Brey, but in a quite different environment – in the middle of a romantic settlement founded by bohemian artists from Schwabing on the banks of Lake Ammersee near Munich – is the summer house of the Munich architect Adelbert Niemeyer. Niemeyer was one of the most creative artists to work under the umbrella of the Deutsche Werkstätten and was one of the founding members of the Deutsche Werkbund in 1907. After that he was occupied chiefly with designs for most of the major German porcelain factories, suppling numerous ideas for tableware and also for lamp stands and other domestic articles, although he was unsuccessful in designing furniture for mass production. His summer house is still furnished throughout with his own designs, which date from 1913, most of which were produced by the Deutsche Werkstätten.

Despite the consciously bohemian lifestyle of their occupants, there is a dignified solemnity to these rooms, apparent in every detail, including the choice of mahogany for the cupboards and the English-inspired mahogany chairs in simple Chippendale style.

Left The seating in a bay of the main living room of Niemeyer's summer house is arranged to make the most of the view towards the lake and also of the morning sun.

The original so-called 'Coco-Cello' on one of the chairs is a reminder that this apparently restrained interior was once the scene of many raucous parties held by Niemeyer for all his local artist friends, whose names are signed on the attached ribbons. The instrument, made from parchment stretched over a coconut, and strung with a single D-string, was played with gusto by Niemeyer who, in founding his Coco-Cello quartet, created one of the most renowned of Munich's bohemian artist societies.

Right Niemeyer used plain local materials and simple shapes when he constructed a covered porch to connect the main house with a small wooden studio for his artist son Paul.

After the First World War German designers found themselves excluded on political grounds from the progress in the decorative and applied arts in Europe, and at home there were no longer wealthy clients wanting villas built and furnished in luxury. But it was not simply a matter of taking on board their clients' reduced financial circumstances and increasingly restricted living spaces: as well as satisfying industry's demands for products suitable for mass production, designers now had also to accommodate new mental attitudes. Wolfgang von Wersin, the director of the Neue Sammlung (New Collection) in Munich, expressed the new mood in these terms: 'The greater the chaos in the outside world, the more people seek clarity, peace and order at home.'

Attempts to confront these new challenges can be seen in the designs of the Werkbund and in the ethos behind the reorganization of the Weimar schools of arts and crafts into the Bauhaus school of design in 1919 by Walter Gropius. He took on to his staff some of the greatest painters, graphic designers and architects of his day, and under them the Bauhaus generated a radical set of ideas. Influenced by the famous declaration of the Viennese designer Adolf Loos that ornament equalled crime, the designs produced by the Werkbund and the Bauhaus – the protagonists of Neue

Sachlichkeit (New Objectivity) – were dictated by function alone. No longer was there any justification for decorative features, unless they were traditionally associated with a particular material or their application facilitated the production process and therefore fitted a practical purpose.

However, although it was at the Bauhaus that Marcel Breuer and Mies van der Rohe established some of the canons of modern furniture design – most notably in Breuer's tubular steel chair, which became an icon of twentieth-century design – little of the art-into-industry process that was promulgated by Gropius and the Werkbund was actually achieved there. While mould-breaking from a design point of view, the Bauhaus proposals were not practical for the average domestic setting of the time. Moreover the Bauhaus model house of 1923, Am Horn, which contained furniture designed by Breuer as well as some useful and innovative labour-saving devices for the housewife, was written off by most critics on aesthetic grounds. The architecture was perceived as a 'white-washed cube', and the stark, purely functional interior was compared to the atmosphere of an operating theatre.

Under the aegis of the Werkbund and organized by van der Rohe, a revolutionary housing development was built at Weissenhof near Stuttgart in 1927. It was the first of its kind to feature fitted kitchens and in-built cupboards. Here white was officially declared the only conceivable colour for the domestic environment: 'Today's white-painted, virtually empty room contains the bare minimum, only such furnishings as are absolutely necessary . . .' An essay of 1930, entitled 'White, all White', describes the new mood of the occupant of such rooms: 'The concept of "Candlelight", those dusky, highly polished interiors, heavy with atmosphere, which once soothed and cradled the human psyche, means nothing to him. He throws open the walls of his house. He looks far beyond their confines for inspiration . . .' This particular German spirit – looking, in a metaphysical way, to grasp the world – was to find its political equivalent a few years later, in 1939.

The general population, however, was not interested in the ideas of Neue Sachlichkeit. 'The masses,' as August Lux, an influential commentator on interior design, ironically put it at the time, felt themselves 'entitled to art too', and they preferred the styles of the past.

Innovative interior design may have lost its pioneering power in Germany. But many of those who were its driving force re-established themselves in the wider world after 1945 from where their influence had far greater effect.

Opposite Marcel Breuer made his 'ti 113' wardrobe in *c.* 1926 when he was head of the furniture workshops at the Bauhaus, which had been driven out of Weimar to Dessau in 1925 under pressure from right-wing forces. The stark linearity of the front almost achieves the formal quality of an abstract painting. The thin red lines set between the smooth-lacquered panels of the doors and drawers serve to emphasize both the cupboard's construction and its function.

Above The interiors of the Weimar Bauhaus workshops were remodelled in the Bauhaus ethos by Oskar Schlemmer, in collaboration with the students of the time, for the school's big open exhibition in 1923. Now the Architecture and Building Faculty of the University of Weimar, the buildings were reconstructed in 1979 according to the Bauhaus plans. The mural on the staircase wall shows figurative, if stylized, elements; the surfaces on the ground floor were decorated with abstract monochrome mortar reliefs. Schlemmer was the director of the Bauhaus mural workshop, the most famous product of which was the monochrome Bauhaus wallpapers of 1929 that were influenced by the work of Kandinsky.

THE RURAL TRADITION

Sentiment and reality through the centuries

Even a small bedroom in a rural dwelling would contain the trappings of the faith that pervaded all aspects of peasant life in the nineteenth century. Thick feather quilts like this were essential for a good night's sleep in Alpine regions.

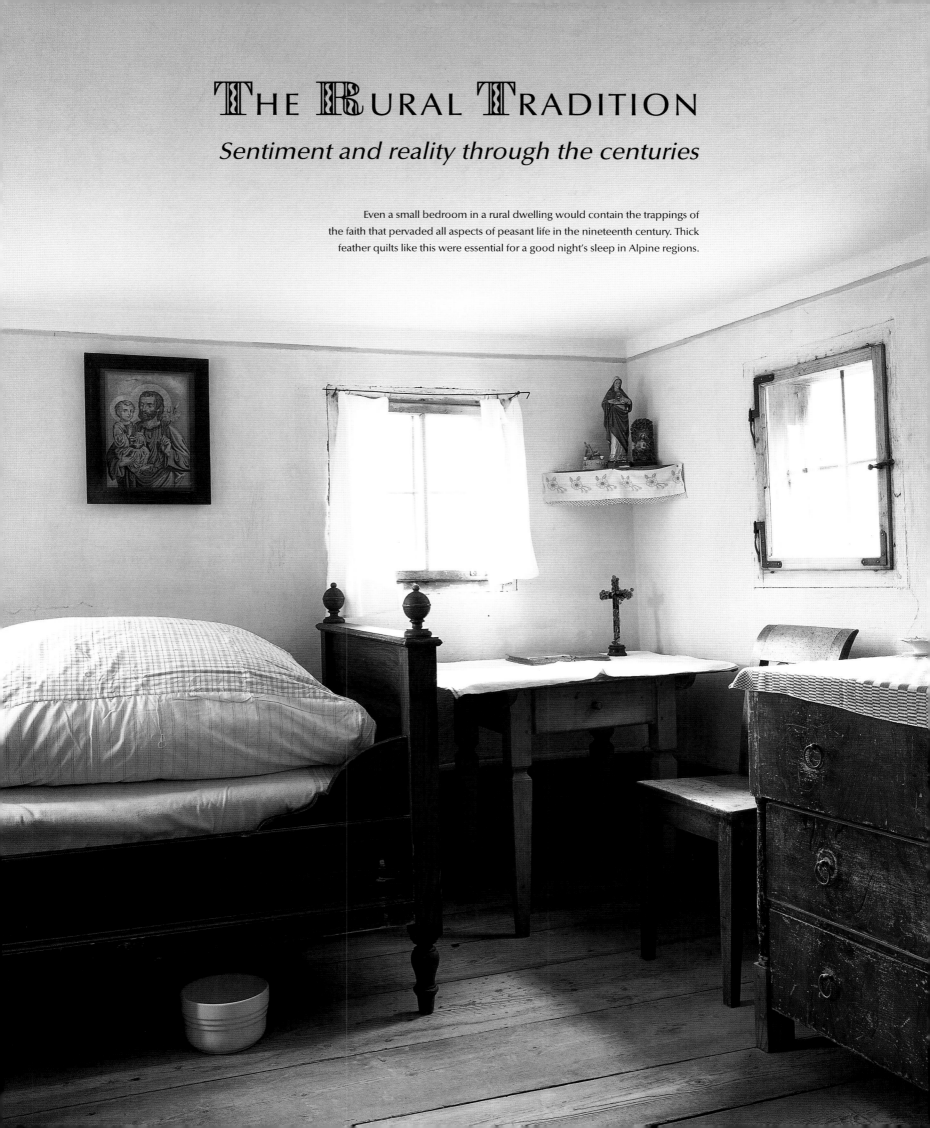

The mistakenly held image of traditional rural life in Germany is of a bucolic idyll. Throughout the world wooden Tyrolean chalets, plump feather quilts and Black Forest cuckoo clocks have become synonymous with the legendary German love of 'hearth and home' – 'Gemütlichkeit'. The myth was fostered by romantic nineteenth-century notions of life on the land and by the reconstructions of farmhouse rooms in many museums that present an overtly idealized picture of rural living conditions. The reality was far tougher and bleaker.

At the beginning of the nineteenth century there was a conscious move to record, systematically, the traditional culture of Bavaria and the Black Forest. Under royal commission, artists travelled all over the regions aiming to capture on paper the long-neglected customs and dress of the indigenous population. Their portrayals revealed an astonishing variety of peasant ways of life and galvanized academics to go into the countryside to document local customs and include dialects – previously scorned as socially unacceptable – in dictionaries. Rural festivals were soon adopted by the general public and deliberately cultivated as an expression of a deep love of the native soil – so much so that many became an important part of a new national identity. The most famous surviving example is the Munich Oktoberfest. Begun in 1810 as a harvest festival and horse-racing event in honour of the future Queen Theresa, it is now regarded as the most authentically German of all festivals and has spawned numerous imitations throughout the world.

Just as members of court society in the eighteenth century had amused themselves by staging imagined versions of 'peasant weddings' in the grounds of their palaces, so nineteenth-century society adopted and adapted those customs and costumes that appealed to their aesthetic sensibilities. Many costumes regarded today as traditionally

Left A strong sense of colour is common to rural interiors of both the north and south. While in north Friesia the walls of the main living room would generally be clad with colourfully glazed ceramic tiles (**top**), in the foothills of the Alps the tradition was for brightly painted furniture (**bottom**). The boldly marbled and decorated bridal cupboards, like this mid-nineteenth-century one from Bavaria, are particularly striking. The diligence of the farmer's wife is evident in the crocheted borders that decorate the display shelves of the cupboard, in the spinning wheel that was used to make hand-spun linen and in the home-made rag rugs on the floor, made from colourful scraps of fabric.

Bavarian are in fact nineteenth-century fabrications that have little to do with the clothing actually worn by the rural population of the past. Because much of the reality was not up to their expectations – either because it was too shabby, or because the peasants for their part were striving to emulate the tastes of the middle classes – the country's intellectuals founded a series of groups dedicated to the revival of what they regarded as an 'authentic' rural way of life.

Part of this movement resulted in traditional farmhouse rooms, or 'Bauernstuben', being installed in all the major decorative arts museums at the end of the century. But despite the undoubtedly good intentions of the curators, these are also products of their time. 'Folk art' became all the rage in certain society circles. Not only did it help to establish vernacular furniture as a new model for manufacturers, but at a time when it was felt that the historicist and foreign influences of previous decades should be abandoned, it was also held up as a shining example of 'authentically German' furnishings to which people should aspire. It was hoped that the discovery of the poetic charm of the old farm dwellings would restore traditional values to the jaded salons of high society.

Symptomatic of this romanticization of rural life was a yawning ignorance of what was in reality a marvellously rich spectrum of cultural forms. From the north coast to the Alps, the enormous diversity of each region is reflected first and foremost in the different types of housing. Although throughout Europe humans and livestock had shared one roof since the Middle Ages – with the exception of the Alpine areas, where family quarters and stables were kept apart – there were differences in how the space was divided up. In the eighteenth and nineteenth centuries the wealthiest peasants were the Friesians, who had colonized and reclaimed the fertile marshland on the lower Elbe and on the North Sea and farmed their own land as 'lords of the

Right The importance of physical comfort, and of getting enough light during the long winters, is evident in the details of these rooms. On top of the cast-iron stove in the living room of this eighteenth-century house in north Friesia (**top**) sits a decorative wooden crate that would have been used for keeping food warm and drying damp cloths. Next to the crate hangs a brass warming pan. The house from the island of Fehmarn (**bottom**) dates from 1746 and has unusually large windows in the gable end. Central dining halls like this, with its floor of simple clay bricks, would usually contain large, impressive cupboards. This one, with painted barley-sugar columns as decoration, is characteristic of the north.

Opposite, left and right This Stube, or living room, in a weaver's cottage in upper Bavaria, is much as it would have been during the late nineteenth century, although the large tiled oven was installed at the beginning of the twentieth century. Around it the family would cook, eat, sleep and dry their washing (**left**). The lying-in bed was in the room, and the family shrine can be seen above the built-in benches around the dining table (**opposite**) in the south-east corner. Animals too had their share of the warmth: beneath the plate rack and behind the curtain (**right**) there once stood a chicken coop.

dikes'. In their large farmhouses, the living area was sited at one end of the elongated hall structure, reached through a long hallway lined on either side by animal stalls. The living area was usually heated by a central stove and was divided into a separate bedchamber, a living room and a strongroom for the storage of dowry chests and other precious items. In the south, where farmyards were sometimes enfolded by two or three buildings (and in lower Bavaria completely enclosed by a quadrant), animals and people might be housed in separate wings.

Until the sixteenth century all rural housing consisted of half-timbered structures, in which the supporting frame of oak or pine beams was filled in either with wattle and daub or – principally in the north – with brickwork. By the end of the eighteenth century this type of timber framing had been largely overtaken by a preference for stone structures, and it was only in the densely forested areas of the Alps and other lower mountain ranges, where wood was in abundant supply, that it continued.

Despite strong regional differences in farmhouse structures, the functions and divisions of the rooms were remarkably similar. In the sixteenth century every house had a room known as the 'Stube'. Sparingly furnished, the Stube was the living room, the focus of the household, the room where the extended family plus farm hands would meet for meals, to rest, to sleep in winter and to dry their washing. The lying-in bed would be set up here to benefit from the warmth, and it was here that families would lay out their dead. There was even room for small animals, such as hens or rabbits, in little stalls under the built-in benches.

Hygiene being almost non-existent, the resulting stench was inescapable – as was recalled by many an eighteenth-century traveller.

Luckily for the occupants, however, the Stube would not have been filled with smoke. Instead of being heated with an open fire, it was warmed by a so-called 'back-loader' or 'side oven' fired from the neighbouring kitchen. The stoves in the south were generally tiled, and in the north would often be clad in cast-iron relief panels. The kitchen, by contrast, was permanently filled with smoke which, until the nineteenth century, would simply be allowed to rise straight up and drift out through gaps in the roof. While the smoke blackened the walls and undoubtedly made life less comfortable, it did have the advantage of drying out and preserving the roof beams as well as the provisions stored in the attic. When in the nineteenth century enclosed chimneys, extending down to the cooking fire, became established, the type of exterior chimney that is still built today was developed: a brick extension built above the ridge of the wooden roof in order to reduce the danger of fire that had been such a constant threat since the Middle Ages.

The family table was usually to be found in the south-east corner of the Stube, and the windows were generally positioned so as to allow in light from both directions. In the Catholic south this corner also served as the family shrine: above the benches there would be a crucifix with a bowl of holy water, and beneath this the farmer would bless the meal and the gathering of family and farm hands would say grace. In numerous picturesque nineteenth-century representations of rural life, this kind of scene was

presented as an illustration of the way that the faith of the peasants permeated every facet of their lives.

The walls of the everyday Stube were generally panelled. In northern Germany, Swabia, the Tyrol and Switzerland, they were panelled all the way up, while in Franconia half-height wainscotting was traditional, with partially stuccoed ceilings. In the coastal areas of the north the inner surface of the outer wall would frequently be clad with glazed tiles imported from Holland, for insulation as well as decoration.

Furnishings were few: in addition to the fixed benches running around the walls the freestanding furniture would generally consist of only a large table and a few simple wooden chairs, some with rush seating. Alcove beds were built into the Stuben of the north, their doors – of either painted wood or linen-hung glass – opening on to the room. These cubbyholes appear tiny to us today but would have slept two or three adults, or as many as five children, in each. Because sleeping habits were different – until the nineteenth century people slept in an almost sitting position – whole families could be accommodated in these alcoves.

In almost all areas of Germany, the better houses would have had a second, 'Gute', Stube, or best parlour. Because they were comparatively little used, they have been better preserved than everyday Stuben. Frequently sited on an upper floor, these rooms were kept for formal use and only entered on special occasions. They were often known by different names in each region: in Franconia, for example, they were called the 'little cabinets', which interestingly reveals an aspiration to a type of room that had been popular with the upper classes since the early sixteenth century. These parlours contained the most valuable of the family's furniture, usually richly painted, including the bridal chest and linen cupboard – pieces which in Bavaria would be paraded through the village on a special 'chamber wagon' on wedding days.

The wealth of Lorens Petersen de Hahn, a successful whaling captain from north Friesia, is evident in the best parlour (**left**) and the living room (**right**) of his house on the island of Sylt which dates from 1699. The sophistication of the decoration – the tortoise-shell effect on the painted panels, the imagery on the ceilings, the religious texts on the alcove-bed doors – is also indicative of the captain's education and elevated social standing. Chests once stood in front of the alcove beds for ease of climbing in and out.
Right top The sloping ceiling of the end wall, covered in tiles from Holland, is typical of the houses of north Friesland. The pair of Staffordshire china dogs would have come from England.

Many of the showpieces for the best parlours in the north must have arrived on boats from Holland: pierced and etched brasses which included long-handled bedwarmers that would be hung up on display; the great brass lids, known as 'fire cuffs', which would be placed over the open flame for safety; and 'pictures' formed by assemblages of ceramic tiles. The most common subjects depicted in tiles were vases of flowers, but images of ships were also a favourite theme, for the Friesian farmers frequently invested their money with the whalers from Glückstadt, adventurers who promised a rich return. Pewter and painted china plates displayed on racks completed the ornament, both in the north and the south.

Below Almost every north German Stube from the eighteenth or nineteenth century contained a triangular cup rack such as the one in this room. Used for the display of precious items, such racks were often decorated with cut-out wooden designs. The square cast-iron stove would have been fed from the kitchen located behind the wall against which the stove stands.

Right In contrast to the homes of the urban middle classes, country dwellings would commonly contain equipment for the manufacture of everyday items and for household chores. Practically every rural Stube contained a spinning wheel and bobbin winder, and the rich ornamentation of a pressing board, like this one hanging beside the wooden wall cupboard, was a matter of pride to the occupants. Through the doors is a glimpse of the best parlour in the house of Lorens Petersen de Hahn. A picture of a whaling boat is hanging on the wall along with a brass warming pan and a triangular sexton case.

The walls of the best parlours were usually highly decorated, with either panels or paintings. Those in some of the Friesian houses had oak panels elaborately carved with birds and flowers, many of which were painted blue to match the colour of the Dutch ceramic tiles. In the extensive fruit-growing areas in the lowlands around Hamburg the preference was for ornately inlaid panels, a form of decoration that originated in Swabia and the Tyrol in the sixteenth and seventeenth centuries. The tenant farmers on the east-facing coasts of the Lower German plains were considerably less wealthy. In place of fine carving, the panels in these houses were generally decorated with cut-out and painted wooden motifs.

There is a long tradition of painted farmhouse walls in both northern and southern Germany. Usually executed by itinerant artists, many murals of quite astounding quality survive from the sixteenth and seventeenth centuries. They are particularly numerous in the area around Salzburg and Berchtesgaden where the cycles of stories from the Bible frescoed on the walls of many churches and monasteries served as rich examples for themes and imagery. In the north, the scenes would often be copied from engravings from illustrated bibles like the edition produced by Matthäus Merian in Strasburg in 1630. The self-educated farmers of Upper Bavaria often chose scenes from the lives of the saints; these would often be combined with leaf and branch patterns and architectural motifs. Sometimes the designs incorporated references to contemporary events. In one particular late-seventeenth-century painting, a townscape features silhouettes which evoke the tents of the Turkish armies that were massing at Germany's borders at that time. The houses on the north Friesian islands such as Sylt, Amrun and Föhr, inhabited mostly by seafarers or those employed in whaling, were frequently decorated with paintings showing scenes from the four corners of the earth – mementoes of their owners' travels.

By far the most popular surfaces for decorative painting, however, were the rural family's proudest possessions: their furniture – chests, cupboards and beds. In the seventeenth century furniture tended to be sparingly decorated, with simple line drawings picked out in black or red on the bare wood. By the eighteenth century it was often covered from top to bottom in colourful designs.

The paints that were used were made from readily available natural products. The most common was casein; this extremely durable compound was derived from quark or skimmed sour milk mixed with lime and then dyed with juices from strawberries, raspberries or blue cornflowers. It was generally painted on to a ground of thin plaster which covered the wooden panelling. This technique continued in all areas of Germany into the nineteenth century, when casein was gradually replaced by oil paints. Most peasant furniture is far more colourful than that of the bourgeoisie or the nobility and in each region its decoration developed into distinctive traditions which lasted well into the nineteenth century.

The textiles of the time – although admittedly rare in the rural household and mostly hand-woven – are also notable for their distinctive patterns and colour combinations. In particular the blue-and-white block-printed cottons of southern Germany are still prized in Bavaria as a naïve variant on the oriental designs that were seen in the wealthier households of the eighteenth century.

Today it is the furniture from Tölz (which lies towards the Alps on the River Isar above Munich) and the areas around the River Inn, and the ornate cupboards of the Tyrol that are regarded as the epitome of German folk-painted furniture. Cupboards generally have two doors, with their fronts divided into four decoratively painted panels. The surrounding mouldings and friezes were either marbled or painted in a single colour. The painters were familiar with the technique of marbling from their experience in

Above and right These murals on the internal walls of a farmhouse in Upper Bavaria are probably the work of an itinerant painter at the end of the seventeenth century. They show a mix of secular and religious images: stag hunting and the figure of St Florian with his wooden bucket of fire-quenching water. Elsewhere in the room is painted the motto 'Spare my house, set fire to another' – a pertinent reminder of one of the principal fears for any farmer.

decorating the many churches of the area in which altars were painted with this effect. The front panels usually depicted religious subjects. Typical of the older furniture in parts of Bavaria are the flaming 'sacred hearts' of Jesus and his mother Mary; and saints with special significance for farming or rural life, such as St Nepomuk, patron saint of bridges and protector of river boats or St Florian, protector of houses against fire, were also popular. In addition, allegories of the four seasons that gave the agricultural year its governing structure were frequently seen, along with a myriad different flower motifs.

But these essentially rural traditions were not untouched by developments in more sophisticated society. The influence of the decorative schemes in court circles is unmistakable, albeit with a distinct time lapse. Thus, for example, the heyday of the so-called 'peasant baroque', with its painted stucco scrolls and mouldings, came at a time

when the aristocracy and the bourgeoisie had long ago left the Baroque and Rococo styles behind and adopted the language of Classicism. The time delay might have made it very difficult to date these splendid farmhouse cupboards, but fortunately they are almost always inscribed with a date, since they were frequently made for a special occasion such as a wedding.

Below and right Bridal, or dowry, furniture like this suite of beds and cupboard was the pride of every Bavarian bride. The surfaces of these items are boldly marbled and decorated with gilded, carved garlands, painted drapery, foliage and bucolic scenes. The cupboard is neatly packed with the young couple's new stock of bed linen, bundles of flax, whole bolts of fresh linen cloth and treasured 'wax sticks' – richly decorated creations made from strands of wax and adorned with images of saints and gold paper decorations. Cupboards like this one, which dates from c. 1850, were paraded through the village for general admiration and were then rarely cleared out or put into everyday use.

Until the 1830s the vividly painted, brightly coloured cupboards were usually set in front of clear white walls, perhaps decorated with stencilled friezes. But during the course of the late eighteenth century a preference grew for brightly coloured walls, often a deep blue and stencilled with a mass of cheerful patterns, and with this came a fashion for pine furniture that was simply treated with a brown wash 'combed' to imitate the grain of a hard wood. It is important to recognize that even in these rural dwellings, walls and furniture were carefully coordinated and there was always a balance between the wall decoration and the furniture. When it is now seen against a plain white background, the brown farmhouse furniture can look drab and gives an utterly misleading impression of the effect of these rural living rooms.

By the end of the century this new style had effectively extinguished the creative powers of the furniture painters. And at the same time that colour began to take over walls, the wood industry began to supply even rural carpenters with ready-made decorative elements such as mouldings or turned applications, and peasant furniture came more into line with bourgeois styles. In Tölz the rural tradition experienced a final flowering. Cupboards were produced here in vast quantities and floated downriver to markets in the Bavarian capital where they were eagerly bought up by the city folk. However, what amounted almost to mass production soon led to slapdash painting and increasingly harsher colours, with the result that their popularity declined, and by 1870 scarcely any were being sold.

Amid the general mood of reform at the start of the twentieth century farmhouse furniture underwent a form of renaissance, being regarded as an expression of the unpretentious tastes of the simple folk. All of a sudden individual items were thought worthy of inclusion in museums, and the ethnographical collections of the big cities began to feature farmhouse interiors as examples of the nation's craft tradition. But it was not until the 1970s that farmhouse furniture came back into fashion as a vital part of the atmospheric decoration of a country house. This happened when increasing prosperity enabled wider

The bedroom of this weaver's house from the Berchtesgaden region of the Alps was connected by a very steep narrow ladder to the Stube below, the hole in the floor also allowing warm air to rise up from the only heated room. The beds have been textured with a special graining technique, giving the simple pine the appearance of a more costly wood.

Left top and bottom From the Bavarian open-air museum on the River Glentleiten there is a wonderful view over the Alpine foothills beyond the Kochelsee. The setting also gives us an inkling of how harsh life must have been in the winter, when so many farms were cut off from the outside world by snow which was sometimes so deep that it was impossible to open the outside doors, and wooden shutters were essential on the ground-floor windows.
Right The dependence of agricultural households on self-sufficiency is evident in the furnishings of their houses: a butter churn in the kitchen and a plentiful supply of wood stacked up outside were essential in both north and south. To ease the hard work of butter-making, the plunger was threaded through a pulley on the ceiling.

sections of society to maintain a rural retreat in addition to a city dwelling. It must be said that there was often little understanding of the true qualities of the now ageing and patina-covered paint effects. Countless cupboards were stripped down to the bare wood in acid baths. This practice went so far that eventually the stripped versions were taken for the authentic style. The furniture industry itself exploited the trend, producing quantities of just this sort of 'genuine' farmhouse furniture from cheap, unfinished pine.

The most convincing picture of the rural existence of the past is now provided by Germany's open-air museums. Situated in beautiful countryside, these institutions are responsible for preserving traditional housing within its original environment in each of their respective regions. Entire houses, complete with their accompanying outhouses, all with their original room arrangements, furnishings and ornament are on display. The most well-known are the Schleswig-Holstein open-air museum in Molfsee near Kiel, the museum village of Cloppenburg south of Oldenburg, the Franconian country museum at Bad Windsheim, and two in Bavaria, at Finsterau in the Bayerischer Wald and in Upper Bavaria on the River Glentleiten near Grossweil on the Kochelsee.

Sylt

Föhr

Amrun

Kiel

Kiel-Molfsee

Lübeck

North Friesia

East Friesia

HAMBURG

Lüneburg

ELBE

WESER

Lower Saxony

HANOVER

BERLIN

Pattensen

Potsdam

Lemgo

Dessau

Saxony

Krefeld

Merseburg

Meissen

DÜSSELDORF

LEIPZIG

COLOGNE

DRESDEN

RHINE

Weimar

Coburg

FRANKFURT

MAIN

Bayreuth

Darmstadt

Würzburg

Franconia

Nuremburg

Stein

Lower Bavaria

Regensburg

DANUBE

STUTTGART

ISAR

Donauwörth

Ulm

Upper Bavaria

Augsburg

MUNICH

Swabia

AMMERSEE

INN

STARNBERGERSEE

Salzburg

Tölz

Murnau

Kochelsee

Innsbruck

The Tyrol

SKETCH MAP SHOWING THE FEATURED LOCATIONS

PLACES TO VISIT
The following museums, castles, palaces and houses that are featured in this book are open to the public; those with an asterisk can only be visited with special prior permission.

IN AND NEAR BAYREUTH
Das Regierungsgebäude des
 Präsidenten von Oberfranken *
Ludwigstrasse 20
95444 Bayreuth
Tel. (00 49) 921/6040

Neues Schloss
Ludwigstrasse 21
95444 Bayreuth
Tel. (00 49) 921/75969-0

Altes und Neues Schloss
Im Park Eremitage
Eremitage
25488 Bayreuth
Tel. (00 49) 921/92561

IN AND NEAR BERLIN
Schloss Pfaueninsel
Pfaueninselchaussee
14109 Berlin (Zehlendorf)
Tel. (00 49) 30/ 8053042

Schloss Tegel *
Adelheidallee 19–21
13507 Berlin-Tegel
Tel. (00 49) 30/ 4343156

IN AND NEAR COBURG
Schloss Ehrenburg
Schlossplatz
96450 Coburg
Tel. (00 49) 9561/8088-0

Schloss Rosenau
96472 Rödental
Tel. (00 49) 9563/4747

NEAR DESSAU
Schloss Wörlitz
Das Gotische Haus
Im Park von Wörlitz
06786 Wörlitz
Tel. (00 49) 34905/4090
 (Palace Musem)
Tel. (00 49) 34905/20302
 (Gothic House Museum)

NEAR INNSBRUCK (AUSTRIA)
Schloss Tratzberg
Gräflich Enzenberg'sche
Gutsverwaltung
6135 Stans
Tel. (00 43) 5242/63566-20

NEAR KIEL
Schleswig-Holsteinisches
 Freilichtmuseum e.V
Hamburger Landstrasse 97
24113 Molfsee
Tel. (00 49) 431/65966-0

IN LEMGO
Städtisches Museum Junkerhaus
Hamelner Strasse 36
32657 Lemgo
Tel. (00 49) 52 61 21 32 76

IN LÜNEBURG
Rathaus Lüneburg
Am Markt 1
21335 Lüneburg
Tel. (00 49) 4131-309230

IN AND NEAR MUNICH (MÜNCHEN)
Lenbachhaus
Luisenstrasse 33
80333 München
Tel. (00 49) 89-23 33 20 00

Schloss Amalienburg
Im Park von Schloss Nymphenburg
80638 München
Tel. (00 49) 89-179080

Villa Stuck
Prinzregentenstrasse 60
81675 München
Tel. (00 49) 89 455 55 10

IN OR NEAR MURNAU
Freilichtmuseum des Bezirks Oberbayern
 an der Glentleiten
An der Glentleiten 4
82439 Grossweil
Tel. (00 49) 8551/185-0

Villa Brey über Eckardt Feuchtmayr *
Oberried 1
82418 Murnau
Tel. (00 49) 884/9120

IN PATTENSEN
Marienburg S.K.H. des Prinzen von
 Hannover *
Pattensen
Tel. (00 49) 5069/407

IN POTSDAM
Neues Palais, Potsdam
Strasse am Neuen Palais
Tel. (00 49) 331 969 4255

Römische Bäder, Potsdam
Tel. (00 49) 331 969 4224

Schloss Charlottenhof, Potsdam
Tel. (00 49) 331 969 4228

Schloss Sanssouci, Potsdam
Tel. (00 49) 331 969 4202

IN SALZBURG (AUSTRIA)
Hohensalzburg Fortress
Mönchsberg 34
5020 Salzburg, Austria
Tel: (00 43) 662/842430-10

IN STEIN
Schloss Faber-Castell *
Nürnberger Str. 2
90546 Stein
Tel. (00 49) 911/99650

IN AND NEAR WEIMAR
Goethes Gartenhaus
Im Park an der Ilm
99423 Weimar
Tel. (00 49) 3643/545375

Schillerhaus
Schillerstr 12
99423 Weimar
Tel. (00 49) 3643/545350

Schloss Tiefurt
Hauptstrasse 14
Weimar-Tiefurt
Tel. (00 49) 3643/545102

Villa Nietzsche
Humboldtstrasse 36
Weimar
Tel. (00 49) 3643/ 545102

Werkstättengebäude des ehemaligen
 Bauhauses, heute Universität Weimar *
Bauhausstrasse 11
99421 Weimar
Tel. (00 49) 3643/580

Wittumspalais
Theaterplatz
99423 Weimar
Tel. (00 49) 3643/545 377-8

SELECT BIBLIOGRAPHY
This selection is intended purely as an introduction to the complex history of German domestic culture, and in compiling it I have attempted to highlight certain previously under-appreciated topics such as textiles and wallpapers. Many of the interiors featured in the book are either little known or at least not documented by independent publications. Where these buildings are under public administration I have referred to the numerous information leaflets or brochures produced by the staff in question.

Horst Apphuhn, Christian von Heusinger, *Riesenholzschnitte und Papiertapeten der Renaissance*, Unterschneidheim 1976

Erich Bachmann und Lorenz Seelig, *Eremitage zu Bayreuth, Amtlicher Führer*, Munich 1987

Erich Bachmann und Alfred Ziffer, *Neues Schloss Bayreuth, Amtlicher Führer*, Munich 1995

Gertrud Benker, *Bürgerliches Wohnen, Städtische Wohnkultur in Mitteleuropa von der Gotik bis zum Jugendstil*, Munich 1984

Jürgen Beyer, *Historische Papiertapeten in Weimar*, Bad Homburg, Leipzig 1993

Das Bleistiftschloß, Familie und Unternehmen Faber-Castell in Stein, Katalog zur Ausstellung, Herausgegeben von Jürgen Franzke, Stein bei Nürnberg, 1986

Wolfgang Braunfels, *Francois Cuvilliés, Der Baumeister der galanten Architektur des Rokoko*, Munich 1986

Herbert Brunner und Lorenz Seelig, *Coburg, Schloss Ehrenburg, Amtlicher Führer*, Munich 1990

Caroline de la Motte Fouqué, *Geschichte der Moden 1785 – 1829*, Herausgegeben von Dorothea Böck, Hanau 1988

Magdalena Droste, *Bauhaus 1919–1933*, Cologne 1990

Sighard Graf Enzenberg, *Schloss Tratzberg, Ein Beitrag zur Kulturgeschichte Tirols*, Innsbruck 1958

Franz von Lenbach, 1836–1904, Katalog zur Ausstellung, Munich 1987

Gartenmöbel des Jugendstils, Künstlermodelle für Beissbarth & Hoffmann, Katalog zur Ausstellung, Karlsruhe 1996

Geschichte des Wohnens, 500–1800 Hausen, Wohnen, Residieren,
  Band 2, Herausgegeben von Ulf Dirlmeier, Stuttgart 1998
Goethe's Gartenhaus im Park an der Ilm, Beiträge zur Baugeschichte,
  Restaurierung und Neueinrichtung, Stiftung Weimarer Klassik, Weimar
  1996
Sonja Günther, *Luxusinterieurs und Arbeitermöbel von der Gründerzeit*
  bis zum 'Dritten Reich', Werkbund-Archiv Band 12, Giessen 1984
Thomas Heyden, *Biedermeier als Erzieher, Studien zum Neubiedermeier*
  in Raumkunst und Architektur 1896–1910, Weimar 1994
Georg Himmelheber, *Kunst des Biedermeier 1815–1835,* Munich 1989
Sigrid Hinz, *Innenraum und Möbel. Von der Antike bis zur Gegenwart,*
  Berlin 1989
Kaiserlicher Kunstbesitz aus dem holländischen Exil Haus Doorn, Katalog
  zur Ausstellung, Berlin 1991
Karl Friedrich Schinkel: A Universal Man, Katalog zur Ausstellung, New
  Haven, London 1991
Karl Junker und das Junkerhaus, Herausgegeben von Regina Fritsch und
  Jürgen Scheffler, Bielefeld 2000
Heinrich Kreisel, Georg Himmelheber, *Die Kunst des deutschen Möbels,*
  Band 1–3, Munich, 1981–1983
Brigitte Langer, *Das Münchner Künstleratelier des Historismus,* Dachau
  1992
Barbara Mundt, *Historismus, Kunstgeschichte zwischen Historismus*
  und Jugendstil, Munich 1981
Adelbert Niemeyer, *Die Arbeit am Gefäss,* Katalog zur Ausstellung,
  Munich 1984
Parkett, Historische Holzfußböden und zeitgenössische Parkettkultur,
  Herausgegeben von Peter Nickl, Munich 1995
Bruno Paul, *Deutsche Raumkunst und Architektur zwischen Jugendstil*
  und Moderne, Katalog zur Ausstellung, Munich 1992
C. Poensgen, *Die Pfaueninsel,* Berlin 1968
Die Raumkunst in Niedersachsen, Die Farbigkeit historischer
  Innenräume, Kunstgeschichte und Wohnkultur, Herausgegeben von
  Rolf-Jürgen Grote und Peter Königfeld, Munich 1991
Paul Ortwin Rave, *Wilhelm von Humboldt und das Schloss zu Tegel,*
  Berlin 1956
Richard Riemerschmid, *Vom Jugendstil zum Werkbund,* Katalog zur
  Ausstellung, Munich, Nuremberg, 1983
Walter Stengel, *Wohnkultur in Berlin und der Mark Brandenburg,* Berlin
  1958
Stoffe und Räume, Eine textile Wohngeschichte der Schweiz, Katalog
  zur Ausstellung, Langenthal 1986
Sabine Thümmler, *Die Geschichte der Tapete, Raumkunst aus Papier,*
  Eurasburg, 1998
Angela Völker, *Die Stoffe der Wiener Werkstätte,* Wien 1990
Weltbild Wörlitz, Entwurf einer Kulturlandschaft, Katalog zur Ausstellung,
  Frankfurt am Main, Stuttgart 1996
Jutta Zander-Seidel, *Textiler Hausrat, Kleidung und Haustextilien in*
  Nürnberg von 1500–1650, Munich 1990
Sabine Ziegler, *Holzvertäfelte Stuben der Renaissance zwischen Main*
  und südlichem Alpenrand, Studien zur Innenarchitektur des 16. und
  17. Jahrhunderts, Frankfurt am Main 1995

Above Schiller's desk at his house on Weimar's Esplanade.
Below The Nietzsche Archive in Weimar, designed by Henry van de Velde.

Left Silver-gilded carving enlivens the walls in the Neue Palais at Potsdam (see page 52).

Right An 'Etruscan' style detail at
Schloss Ehrenburg in Coburg (see
page 86).

Left A dog kennel from the Alpine region of Bavaria (see page 184).

AUTHOR'S ACKNOWLEDGEMENTS

The help and advice of numerous people and institutions have been instrumental in bringing this book to publication. First and foremost I would like to thank the owners of the private houses for allowing us to photograph interiors which in many cases have never before been revealed to the public, and I am equally indebted to the personnel of the many publicly administered buildings who gave me their help. Among those I must name are: Ulrich Graf Goëss-Enzenberg, Schloss Tratzberg; S.K.H. Prinz Ernst August von Hannover, Herzog zu Braunschweig und Lüneburg, Marienburg; Eckardt Feuchtmayr, Villa Brey; Familie von Heinz, Schloss Tegel; Familie P. Niemeyer, Villa Niemeyer; Frau Dr Gerda Carl, Villa Carl; Dr Ch Graf Douglas, Prof Dr W. Baer, Berlin; Dr M. Eissenhauer, Coburg; Frau Dr H. Graf, Munich; Dr P. Pinneau, Kulturreferat der Stadt Munich; Dr Graham Dry, Johann Graf Wilczek, Vienna; Dr H. Beyer, Festungsverwaltung Hohensalzburg, Dr B. Göres, Direktor der Stiftung Preussische Schlösser und Gärten; Dr Ch. Graf Pfeil und Dr A. Miller, Bayerische Verwaltung der Staatlichen Schlösser, Gärten und Seen; Frau Dr Johanna zu Eltz-Oraschkoff, Städtische Galerie im Lenbachhaus, Dr Hans Angerer, Regierungspräsident von Oberfranken; H. Eiselt, Oberbürgermeisterbüro Lüneburg; Dr Louft-Gaude, Freilichtmuseum Kiel Molfsee; Frau Lobenhofer, Freilichtmuseum des Bezirks Oberbayern, An der Glentleiten; Dr Gert-Dieter Ulferts, Staatliche Kunstsammlungen Weimar; Frau Dr D. Hülsenbeck, Schloss Faber-Castell; J. Scheffler, Museumsleiter Lemgo; many others were also very helpful.

I am also grateful to the translator Niccola Shearman and for the kind and competent guidance of the editor Tristram Holland. Last but not least my heartfelt thanks go to the photographers Barbara and René Stoeltie, who have accompanied me throughout Germany on the sometimes tiring, always stimulating and occasionally adventurous search for authentic German interiors. *Sigrid Sangl*

PUBLISHER'S ACKNOWLEDGMENTS

C=centre, L=left, R=right, A=above, B=below
The publisher would like to thank the following who have kindly given us
  permission to reproduce pictures of properties in their care:
Archiv & Sammlung Graf Faber-Castell 134L, 124, 133R, 144–151
Bayerisches National Museum, Munich 11R, 16
Bayerische Verwaltung der Staalichen Schlösser, Garten und Seen:
    Amalienburg 6C, 28, 29, 31R, 34–37; Neues Schloss 31L, 32, 42, 43, 44, 45;
    Eremitage 38–41; Schloss Ehrenburg 6R, 30, 86–89, 187, 190 and Schloss
    Rosenau 2, 3, 57A, 90–93
Burgverwaltung Salzburg 8/9, 11L, 20–23
Dr Gerda Carl 152B, 154–157
Huis Doorn 113R, 125–127
Family Eckardt Feuchtmayr 152A, 158–161
Freilichtmuseum des Bezirks Oberbayern An der Glentleiten 7R, 168, 169, 172,
    173, 178, 182/183, 184, 191
Count Ulrich von Goëss-Enzenberg 6L, 10R, 12–19
S.K.H. Prinz von Hannover, Herzog zu Braunschweig und Lüneburg 7L,
    110–112, 114–119, 121
Family von Heinz 56A, 71–77
Kulturstiftung Dessau-Wörlitz; Schloss Mosikgau 31C, 33;
    Schloss Wörlitz 58–63
Museum Villa Stuck 130, 131, 132C, 134, 135
Regierung von Oberfranken 1, 132R, 133L, 140–143
Schleswig-Holsteinisches Freilichtmuseum Kiel-Molfsee 170, 171, 174–177,
    180, 181, 185
© Copyright photograph Die Neue Sammlung, Staatliches Museum für
    angewandte Kunst, Munich 166
Stadtverwaltung Lüneburg 10L, 24–27
Städtische Galerie im Lenbachhaus, Munich, 120, 122, 123
Städtisches Museum Lemgo (Junkerhaus) 128, 129
Stiftung Preussische Schlösser und Garten; Charlottenhof 4, 5, 78–85, 192;
    Neues Palais 50–53, 189; Römische Bäden 56B, 70; Pfaueninsel 64–69;
    Sanssouci Palais 46–49
Stiftung Weimarer Klassik; Goethes Gartenhaus 94–97; Nietzsche Archiv 7C,
    132L, 136–139, 188B; Schillerhaus 54, 55, 98–103, 105 188A; Schloss Tiefurt
    57B, 104, 106, 107; Wittumspalais 108, 109
Weimar University (formerly Bauhaus) 167

Map on page 186 Joanna Logan © Frances Lincoln 2000

A winter view from the summer palace of Charlottenhof towards one of the bronze gazelles by Wilhelm Wolff, 1846, in Sanssouci Park, Potsdam.